ROBERT LOUIS STEVENSON
and his world

DAVID DAICHES

ROBERT LOUIS STEVENSON
and his world

THAMES AND HUDSON

LONDON

TO MY GRANDCHILDREN
RACHEL, GOWAN, DAVEY, ANNA,
and GIDEON

As from the house your mother sees
You playing round the garden trees,
So you will see, if you will look
Through the windows of this book,
Another child, far, far away,
And in another garden, play.
But do not think you can at all,
By knocking on the window, call
That child to hear you. He intent
Is all on his play-business bent.
He does not hear; he will not look,
Nor yet be lured out of this book.
For, long ago, the truth to say,
He has grown up and gone away,
And it is but a child of air
That lingers in the garden there.

From Robert Louis Stevenson,
A Child's Garden of Verses

Printed in Great Britain by
Jarrold and Sons Ltd, Norwich

ISBN 0 500 130450

The Old Town, Edinburgh, seen from Princes Street. This photograph, taken in 1866, shows Waverley Station as it was during Louis's boyhood. 'They lean over the great bridge which joins the New Town with the Old – that windiest spot, or high altar, in this northern temple of the winds – and watch the trains smoking out from under them and vanishing into the tunnel on a voyage to brighter skies.' (*Edinburgh: Picturesque Notes.*)

ROBERT LEWIS BALFOUR STEVENSON was born on 13 November 1850 at 8 Howard Place, Edinburgh. Howard Place, a small street of unpretentious yet elegant Georgian houses built in the 1820s in a late phase of the development of Edinburgh's New Town, lies just north of the Water of Leith, a section of the longer (and slightly later) Inverleith Row, which runs north towards Granton and the Firth of Forth. In 1853 the family moved across the way to 1 Inverleith Terrace, a larger house, no longer in existence, on a street that comes into Inverleith Row at right angles from the west. Though larger, the new house was damp and more exposed than the Stevensons' former home, and medical advice suggested that the small boy's frequent coughs and fevers required a more salubrious home; the result was that in 1856 the Stevensons moved again, this time to 17 Heriot Row, a substantial, well-built terrace house in a south-facing street built in the first decade of the nineteenth century as the first part of Edinburgh's well-planned northern or second New Town.

Stevenson thus grew up in Georgian Edinburgh, amid elegant streets inhabited by genteel professional families. To the north, the city sloped down to the Firth of Forth, with the hills of Fife clearly visible, when not obscured by rain or sea fog, from the corner of Heriot Row and Howe Street, only a few paces from the Stevenson house. To the south, across Queen Street Gardens and the symmetrically planned parallel thoroughfares of Queen Street, George Street and Princes Street, lay Princes Street Gardens, dominated by the Castle which guarded the picturesque and slum-filled Old Town. At the east end of Princes Street, where the North Bridge joined the Old Town with the New, lay Waverley Station, and the young Stevenson would watch from the bridge

Louis's birthplace in Georgian
Edinburgh: 8 Howard Place.

as the trains puffed out, yearning to join the travellers in adventuring to strange new places. Further east lay Holyrood and the lion shape of Arthur's Seat. To the west lay the little old Dean Village, unspoilt in its hollow by the Water of Leith. One could follow this stream to the north-west suburb of Colinton, where the boy's grandfather was minister, and there one was within a stone's throw of the Pentland Hills, which early laid a hold on his imagination. City elegance, city adventure, city squalor, but also streams and hills and lochs, and the sea never far away. Stevenson, who was to grow up to become above all things a novelist of *place*, fitting action to local atmosphere with a remarkable sense of topographical appropriateness, savoured as a boy all these aspects of his native city, and they remained always in his imagination.

Called Robert after his paternal grandfather and Lewis (the name actually used) after his maternal grandfather, the child did not long remain 'Lewis', for his Tory father took a violent dislike to a radical named Lewis and changed the spelling of his son's name to 'Louis' to prevent even an orthographical association with the man. But, though spelt in the French manner, the name was always pronounced with the final 's' sounded. So though we may now call him Louis, the reader must mentally sound it as 'Lewis' if he is to call him as he was called by his parents and friends.

Louis was the only child of Thomas Stevenson and Margaret Isabella Balfour. Thomas was a lighthouse engineer, son, grandson and great-grandson of lighthouse engineers; he was born at Edinburgh in 1818. His father, Robert Stevenson, had built the lighthouse on the Bell Rock, his masterpiece and an engineering triumph, and Thomas himself had, in the words of Louis's memoir of him, 'served under his brother Alan in the building of Skerryvore, the noblest of all extant deep-sea lights; and, in conjunction with his brother David, he added two – the Chickens and the Dhu Heartach – to that small number of man's extreme outposts in the ocean'. He was also a harbour engineer, but, again in his son's words, 'the great achievement of his life was . . . in optics as applied to lighthouse illumination'. The most important of his inventions was a revolving light, on which, as on his other inventions, he never took out a patent, so that 'my father's instruments enter anonymously into a hundred light-rooms, and are passed anonymously over in a hundred reports, where the least considerable patent would stand out and tell its author's story'. He prospered in his profession, and by the time of his son's birth was a substantial Edinburgh citizen. Louis has left a description of his father's character:

He was a man of a somewhat antique strain: with a blended sternness and softness that was wholly Scottish and at first somewhat bewildering; with a profound essential melancholy of disposition and (what often accompanies it) the most humorous geniality in company; shrewd and childish; passionately attached, passionately prejudiced; a man of many extremes, many faults of temper and no very stable foot-hold for himself among life's troubles. Yet he was a wise adviser; many men, and these not inconsiderable, took counsel with him habitually. . . . He had never any Greek; Latin he happily re-taught himself after he had left school where he was a mere consistent idler: happily, I say, for Lactantius, Vossius, and Cardinal Bona were his chief authors. . . . Another old theologian, Brown of Wamphray, was often in his hands. When he was indisposed, he had two books, *Guy Mannering* and *The Parent's Assistant* [Maria Edgeworth's volumes of children's stories], of which he never wearied. He was a strong Conservative, or, as he preferred to call himself, a Tory; except in so far as his views were modified by a hot-headed chivalrous sentiment for women. He was actually in favour of a marriage law under which any woman might have a divorce for the asking, and no man on any ground whatever; and the same sentiment found another expression in a Magdalen Mission in Edinburgh, founded and largely supported by himself. This was but one of the many channels of his public generosity; his private was equally unstrained. The Church of Scotland, of which he held the doctrines (though in a sense of his own) and to which he bore a clansman's loyalty, profited often by his time and money; and though, from a morbid sense of his own unworthiness, he would never consent to be an office-bearer, his advice was often sought, and he served the Church on many committees. What he perhaps valued highest in his work were his contributions to the defence of Christianity. . . .

The drawing-room of 17 Heriot Row.

The 'blended sternness and softness' to which Louis refers manifested itself in a variety of ways. Thomas had been, again in his son's words, an 'idle eager sentimental youth'. He had a romantic imagination, and put himself to sleep nightly with stories of 'ships, roadside inns, robbers, old sailors, and commercial travellers before the era of steam'. He would entertain his small son during the latter's many nights of sickness with similar tales, and later when Louis made up his own first tales of romantic adventure Thomas was keenly and critically interested. He was fond of dogs, believing that they had souls, and would make friends with any stray he met in the street. He also had a habit of accosting school-children carrying their loads of books to or from school and advising them merrily to learn only what they liked or even, if they preferred, to have nothing to do with book-learning at all. Yet he was a nervous, intense man, deeply committed to Christian theology as he understood it, and when eventually Louis lost his faith in that theology the confrontation between father and son was hard and bitter.

But little Louis, or Lou, or 'Smout' (which in Scots variously means salmon fry, a small speckled trout, or, by extension, any small creature), as first his father and then other members of his family called him, saw mostly his father's softer side. There was a great deal of affectionate banter in their relationship, which continued right through Louis's school-days. When he was fifteen, on a visit to Torquay, he wrote to his father asking for cash, addressing him as 'Respected Paternal Relative' and pointing out that since he had got through the immediately preceding winter without serious illness, thus saving his father large sums in drugs and physicians' fees, he deserved remuneration. 'I appeal to your charity, I appeal to your generosity, I appeal to your accounts, I appeal, in fine, to your purse.' He concludes: 'My sense of generosity forbids the receipt of more – my sense of justice forbids the receipt of less – than half a crown.' It is important to remember this side of the relationship between father and son when we come to later developments.

Mrs Thomas Stevenson, Margaret or simply Meg, was the youngest of the thirteen children of the Reverend Dr Lewis Balfour, minister at Colinton, who was himself the younger son of John Balfour of Pilrig and grandson of James Balfour of Pilrig, Professor of Moral Philosophy at Edinburgh University. (Louis introduces James Balfour into *Catriona*.) James married into the Aberdeenshire family of Elphinstone, but his wife's mother was an Elliot of Minto and thus of Border descent, which led Louis to claim that in the person of an ancestor he had 'shaken a spear in the Debateable land and shouted the slogan of the Elliots'. Lewis Balfour married a daughter of the George Smith, minister of Galston, whom Burns ironically castigates in 'The Holy Fair' for being more concerned with good works than with faith. Thus Meg was a daughter of the manse on both sides.

She was only nineteen when she married in 1848, tall, fair, graceful and lively, and her relationship with little Louis is vividly illustrated by an anecdote he told in later life: 'I remember with particular pleasure running upstairs in Inverleith Terrace with my mother – herself little more than a girl – to the top flat of this our second house, both of us singing as best we could "We'll all go up to Gatty's room, to Gatty's room, etc.," *ad lib.*; Gatty being

Louis with his mother: a photograph taken in 1854.

8

contracted for Grandpapa, my mother's father, who was coming to stay with us.' She was tolerant and good-natured, and her temperament combined gaiety with simple but real piety. Though she outlived her son, her health during Louis's childhood was uncertain, and Louis's first visit abroad – to the Riviera in 1863 – was with his mother for the sake of her health. She was immensely proud of her son from his earliest infancy, and recorded in her diary evidence of his precocity from the time he was two. On 26 July 1853 she noted: 'Smout's favourite occupation is making a church; he makes a pulpit with a chair and a stool; reads sitting, and then stands up and sings by turns.' When he was just three she recorded that they had a guest for dinner and 'Smout recited the first four lines of "On Linden" in great style, waving his hand and making a splendid bow at the end. This is Cummie's teaching'.

'Cummie' (or 'Cummy') was Alison Cunningham, who came to look after Louis when he was eighteen months old, serving as the nanny that prosperous Victorian families engaged for their children as a matter of course. She played a very special part in Louis's life, and he never forgot her. The little boy, with his persistent colds and sore throats and fevers, needed careful tending, and Cummie tended him devotedly. When he grew up he dedicated to her *A Child's Garden of Verses*, poems based on still vivid childhood memories:

Alison Cunningham ('Cummie') in old age.

> For the long nights you lay awake
> And watched for my unworthy sake:
> For your most comfortable hand
> That led me through the uneven land:
> For all the story-books you read:
> For all the pains you comforted:
> For all you pitied, all you bore,
> In sad and happy days of yore: –
> My second Mother, my first Wife,
> The angel of my infant life –
> From the sick child, now well and old,
> Take, nurse, the little book you hold!

'My recollections of the long nights when I was kept awake by coughing,' Louis wrote in an autobiographical fragment, 'are only relieved by the thought of the tenderness of my nurse and second mother (for my first will not be jealous), Alison Cunningham. She was more patient than I can suppose of an angel; hours together she would help and console me . . . till the whole sorrow of the night was at an end with the arrival of the first of that long string of country carts, that in the dark hours of the morning, with the neighing of the horses, the cracking of the whips, the shouts of drivers, and a hundred other wholesome notes, creaked, rolled, and pounded past my window.' There is another passage of autobiography which vividly shows the parts respectively played by his nurse and his father:

My ill-health principally chronicles itself by the terrible long nights that I lay awake, troubled continuously by a hacking, exhausting cough, and praying for sleep or morning from the bottom of my shaken little body. I principally connect these nights, however, with our third house, in Heriot Row; and cannot mention them without a grateful testimony to the unwearied sympathy and long-suffering displayed to me on a hundred such occasions by my good nurse. . . . How well I remember her lifting me out of bed, carrying me to the window, and showing me one or two lit windows up in Queen Street across the dark belt of gardens; where also, we told each other, there might be sick little boys and their nurses waiting, like us, for the morning. Other night scenes connected with my ill-health were the little sallies of delirium that used to waken me out of a feverish sleep, in such agony of terror as, thank God, I have never suffered since. My father had generally to come up and sit by my bedside, and feign conversations with guards or coachmen or innkeepers, until I was gradually quieted and brought to myself; but it was long after one of those paroxysms before I could bear to be left alone.

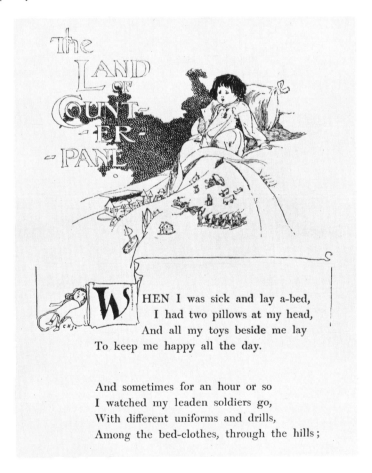

Louis's ill-health as a child is poignantly suggested by this page from an early edition of *A Child's Garden of Verses*.

Some of Louis's toy lead soldiers.

Cummie presented a peculiarly Scottish blend of strong imagination, a great love of rhetoric and dramatic speech, and a strict adherence to the narrow Covenanting version of Scottish Presbyterianism. Playing-cards were the devil's picture-books and both novels (as distinct from moral tales) and the theatre were anathema. Yet she both danced and sang to Louis, even if the songs were mostly metrical versions of the Psalms, and read to him with great dramatic power from the Bible and Bunyan and accounts of persecuted

Covenanters. 'It's *you* that gave me a passion for the drama, Cummie,' Louis
told her, the last time they ever saw each other, in a room full of people, as she
herself recollected. 'Me, Master Lou,' she replied; 'I never put foot inside a
playhouse in my life.' 'Ay, woman,' said Louis; 'but it was the grand
dramatic way ye had of reciting the hymns.'

Cummie would read aloud from *Cassell's Family Paper*, but if she found
that one of the stories looked like turning into a 'regular novel' she would drop
it, little Louis giving, as he recalled later, his 'pious approval'. 'Yet neither
she nor I were wholly stoical; and when Saturday came round, we would
study the windows of the stationer, and try to fish out of the subsequent wood-
cuts and their legends the further adventures of our favourites.' The small boy's
dramatic sense was fed more directly by 'Skelt's Juvenile Drama', scenes and
characters for a toy theatre sold, together with the play-book, at a stationer's
shop at the corner of Antigua Street and Union Street, on Leith Walk. Louis
recalled his fascination with 'Skeltery' in his essay 'A Penny Plain and Two
Pence Coloured', which he wrote in 1883 and included in *Memories and
Portraits* in 1887. 'In the Leith Walk window, all the year round, there stood
displayed a theatre in working order, with a "forest set", a "combat", and a

Pub.d by E. SKELT.   No 2

few "robbers carousing" in the slides; and below and about, dearer tenfold to me! the plays themselves, those budgets of romance, lay tumbled one upon another. Long and often have I lingered there with empty pockets. One figure, we shall say, was visible in the first plate of characters, bearded, pistol in hand, or drawing to his ear the clothyard arrow; I would spell the name: was it Macaire, or Long Tom Coffin, or Grindoff, 2nd dress? O, how I would long to see the rest! how – if the name by chance were hidden – I wondered in what play he figured, and what immortal legend justified his attitude and strange apparel!' Skelt's world of cheap melodrama stamped his childish imagination. But that imagination was also stimulated, in a quite different way, by the sights and sounds of his native city.

Among those sights and sounds were those associated with his grand‑father's manse at Colinton, now an integral part of the city of Edinburgh but then a village nestling in a hollow just north of the Pentlands. Until Dr Balfour's death in Louis's tenth year, the boy stayed frequently at the manse to play with cousins and regain health. 'Out of my reminiscences of life in that dear place,' he wrote in 1873, 'all the morbid and painful elements have disappeared. I remember no more nights of storm; no more terror or sickness.

Louis's youthful imagination was fired by the coloured sheets of cut‑out actors (such as this one, devoted to smugglers), published by E. Skelt for use in toy theatres. (*Opposite*) The stationer's shop in Leith Walk where Louis bought these sheets.

Beyond a thunder-storm when I was frightened, after a half make-believe fashion, and huddled with my cousins underneath the dining-room table; and a great flood of the river, to see which my father carried me wrapped in a blanket through the rain; I can recall nothing but sunshiny weather. That was my golden age: *et ego in Arcadia vixi*.' In a later essay, also included in *Memoirs and Portraits*, entitled simply 'The Manse', he recalled the place again:

It was a place in that time like no other: the garden cut into provinces by a great hedge of beech, and overlooked by the church and the terrace of the churchyard, where the tombstones were thick, and after nightfall 'spunkies' might be seen to dance, at least by children; flower-pots lying warm in sunshine; laurels and the great yew making elsewhere a pleasing horror of shade; the smell of water rising from all round, with an added tang of papermills; the sound of water everywhere, and the sound of mills – the wheel and the dam singing their alternate strain; the birds on every bush and from every corner of the overhanging woods pealing out their notes until the air throbbed with them; and in the midst of this, the manse.

There he played with his cousins, on grass and by water; there they frightened themselves with stories of a dead man watching them from the churchyard over the wall; there young Lou stalked imaginary game with a toy gun on the lawn, played pirates by the mill-stream, and on several occasions tried to invoke the Devil with incantations learned from Skelt's *Juvenile Drama of Der Freischütz*.

To the south of Colinton one looked up to the Pentland Hills, but it was not until the summer of 1867 that the Stevensons took a country cottage, largely for summer use, in the village of Swanston, at the eastern end of the Pentlands, and this gave Louis the opportunity to explore the hills intimately.

Edinburgh, seen in the distance from the Pentland Hills: one of the illustrations from the first edition of *Edinburgh : Picturesque Notes*.

The village of Colinton, as it was in about 1880.

He described Swanston and its environs in his essay 'To the Pentland Hills', one of a series on Edinburgh that he wrote for *The Portfolio* in 1878 and which appeared in book form in 1879 as *Edinburgh: Picturesque Notes*:

The hamlet . . . is one of the least considerable of hamlets, and consists of a few cottages on a green beside a burn. Some of them (a strange thing in Scotland) are models of internal neatness; the beds adorned with patch-work, the shelves arrayed with willow-pattern plates, the floors and tables bright with scrubbing or pipeclay, and the very kettle polished like silver. . . . But hills and hill people are not easily sophisticated; and if you walk out here on a summer Sunday, it is as like as not the shepherd may set his dogs upon you. But keep an unmoved countenance; they look formidable at the charge, but their hearts are in the right place; and they will bark and sprawl about you on the grass, unmindful of their master's excitations.

Kirk Yetton forms the north-eastern angle of the range; thence, the Pentlands trend off to south and west. From the summit you look over a great expanse of champaign sloping to the sea and behold a large variety of distant hills. There are the hills of Fife, the hills of Peebles, the Lammermoors and the Ochils, more or less mountainous in outline, more or less blue with distance. Of the Pentlands themselves, you see a field of wild heathery peaks with a pond gleaming in the midst; and to that side the view is as desolate as if you were looking into Galloway or Applecross. To turn to the other, is like a piece of travel. Far out in the lowlands Edinburgh shows herself, making a great smoke on clear days and spreading her suburbs about her for miles; the Castle rises darkly in the midst; and close by, Arthur's Seat makes a bold

Swanston Cottage, where the Stevenson family spent much of their time during the summers from 1867.

figure in the landscape. All around, cultivated fields, and woods, and smoking villages, and white country roads, diversify the uneven surface of the land. Trains crawl slowly abroad upon the railway lines; little ships are tacking in the Firth; the shadow of a mountainous cloud, as large as a parish, travels before the wind. . . . The spiry, habitable city, ships, the divided fields, and browsing herds, and the straight highways, tell visibly of man's active and comfortable ways; and you may be never so laggard and never so unimpressionable, but there is something in the view that spirits up your blood and puts you in the vein for cheerful labour.

By the time he entered Edinburgh University in November 1867 Louis possessed this scene, not merely as a series of vividly etched visual memories but as part of his deep sense of human landscape against which human dramas are acted out. The dramas may at first have come from 'Skelt's Juvenile Drama', but the landscape was real and genuinely related in his imagination to the ways in which human labour is carried out and human wants make themselves felt. Young Louis had met poverty and drunkenness in Edinburgh streets, as well as shepherds on the Pentlands, and he remembered them equally. A late memory of Edinburgh written in distant Samoa recalls not only the beauty of 'the august airs of the castle on its rock, nocturnal passages of lights and trees, the sudden song of the blackbird in a suburban lane, rosy and dusky winter sunsets, the uninhabited splendours of the early dawn, the building up of the city on a misty day, house above house, spire above spire, until it was received into a sky of softly glowing clouds', but also 'shabby suburban tan/fields, rainy beggarly slums, taken in at a gulp nigh forty years ago, and surviving today, complete sensations, concrete, poignant and essen/ tial to the genius of the place'. For a novelist who was to become deeply involved with the genius of place, Stevenson had an appropriate childhood in Edinburgh. He was to travel often and far, and enrich his imagination with a great variety of scenes, but Edinburgh and its environs lay perpetually in his mind as a touchstone of what a novelist's scene ought to be, and he returned to them in his two last novels, left unfinished at his death.

Young Louis early showed signs both of a novelist's imagination and of a writer's obsession with writing. In January 1855 his mother recorded in her diary that 'when made to wear a shawl above his sword, he was in distress for fear it would not look like a soldier, and then said, "Do you think it will look like a night-march, mama?"' and a few weeks later he dreamed that he heard 'the noise of pens writing'. When he was barely six years old he dictated to his mother a 'History of Moses', an amusing mixture of accurately remembered biblical language and a child's narrative style, and followed this up the next year with 'The Book of Joseph, by R.L.B.S., the author of "A History of Moses"', written (or rather dictated) in a similar manner. He used to compose and recite to himself in bed what he called 'songstries', at least one of which was taken down by his proud father standing outside the bedroom door. The one that survives is a curious pious rhapsody about angels and devils and Christ, an aspect of the somewhat histrionic religiosity that Louis demonstrated as a very small boy. During his schooldays Louis was continually producing home-made magazines single-handed. When he was barely sixteen he wrote an account of the Pentland Rising of 1666, an unsuccessful attempt by an army of Covenanters to attack the Government forces that harassed them; it is a rather dull narrative, but it draws intelligently on original sources. His father had it printed in a small edition at his own expense.

There was little doubt of Louis's precocity. He lived much in his imagination, partly the result of his frequent illnesses. He was a solitary boy, apart from summers at Colinton Manse playing with his cousins, and became adept at making up games for himself. He started attending a preparatory school at Cannonmills in the autumn of 1857, being duly taken and called for by Cummie, but his frequent colds and other illnesses made his attendance fairly sporadic, while Cummie's insistence on his wrapping up well (and, if the weather was wet, on changing his socks for him on arrival in the presence of his schoolmates) was not calculated to make him a school hero. In 1861 he entered the Edinburgh Academy, the day-school for the education of gentlemen's sons that Sir Walter Scott had helped to found in 1824. In 1863, when his parents wintered at Menton for the sake of his mother's health, he was briefly at a boarding-school at Spring Grove, Isleworth, in Middlesex, where a maternal aunt lived, whose sons attended the same school. He wrote to his mother from the school on 12 November 1863 in a rather desperate French ('Je suis presque driven mad par une bruit terrible tous les garçons kik up comme grand un bruit qu'il est possible') and added a note to his father which said simply: 'My dear papa, you told me to tell you whenever I was miserable. I do not feel well, and I wish to get home. Do take me with

Advocate's Close, Edinburgh, part of the 'beggarly slums' which Louis was to recall in a memoir towards the end of his life.

The Edinburgh Academy, which Louis entered in 1861. 'I blush to own I am an Academy boy; it seems modern, and smacks not of the soil.' (Letter from Louis to Alexander Ireland, March 1882.)

you.' He joined his mother on the Riviera at the end of the term and never returned to Spring Grove. From 1864 to 1867 he attended a school near his home in Frederick Street, Edinburgh. Another pupil of this school later recollected that its principal feature was the absence of homework, two or three hours of afternoon school being set aside for preparation of the next day's lessons. This meant that Louis had more leisure after school than most schoolboys, and he spent his free time writing, including a considerable amount of doggerel verse in octosyllabic lines.

He was, of course, also reading. He had been introduced to Shakespeare very young, when his mother read *Macbeth* aloud to him. He discovered Dumas in 1863. He first discovered Scott's novels in his father's library, and though the first time he tried *Rob Roy* he stuck, he soon became an enthusiast, for that as for others of Scott's novels. He developed at a surprisingly early age an admiration for Thackeray's *Book of Snobs*, and wrote a description of the inhabitants of Peebles in that style before he was thirteen. He also read the works of the Covenanting historians such as Robert Wodrow's *History of the Sufferings of the Church of Scotland* and *Analecta, or Materials for a History of Remarkable Providences* and James Kirkton's *Secret and True History of the Church of Scotland*. 'My style is from the Covenanting writers,' he wrote to J. M. Barrie from Samoa in 1893. 'When I was a child, and indeed until I was a man, I consistently read Covenanting books,' he says in the same letter, and adds that recently he has been reading little else. This is not a negligible aspect of Stevenson's imagination or of his style.

In spite of his frequent illnesses, Louis managed to acquire some physical skills. He learned to ride in the summers of 1865 and 1866. On family holidays at North Berwick and elsewhere he learned to cope with sand and sea, and became an adept at 'crusoeing', which he described as 'a word that covers

The sands at North Berwick.

Thomas and Margaret Stevenson,
with Louis and (far right) Cummie.
(*Left*) Louis, aged ten, on a donkey.

all extempore eating in the open air: digging, perhaps, a house under the margin of the links, kindling a fire of the sea-ware and cooking apples there'. He was also a leader in the romantically meaningless activity of lantern-bearing, which consisted in walking alone on a dark night with a bull's-eye lantern buttoned under your top-coat and saying 'Have you got your lantern?' to any of your companions whom you met. (This indicates that he did eventually acquire some playmates at school.) Louis was abroad several times with his parents before his university days, but there is little evidence that foreign travel made much impression on him at this stage, though he later told a friend that he had adored the River Rhône since he first saw it from the train at the age of twelve.

Thomas Stevenson was proud of his son's early writing, and encouraged him in his juvenile literary endeavours, but it never occurred to him that Louis would want to engage in writing as a profession. Writing was an excellent avocation for a gentleman with a proper means of livelihood elsewhere but not, in the view of Thomas and of many genteel inhabitants of the Edinburgh of his day, a respectable or an economically dependable full-time pursuit. Louis was expected to follow the family tradition and become a lighthouse engineer. He was nearly seventeen (not unduly young for the time) when he entered Edinburgh University, already determined in his own mind to be a writer but willing for a while to accept his father's view, so that as well as the Latin class he attended in a desultory way courses in 'natural philosophy' (physics), mathematics and civil engineering. But he was never a serious student. 'For my own part,' he wrote later in *An Apology for Idlers*, 'I have attended a good many lectures in my time. I still remember that the spinning of a top is a case of Kinetic Stability. I still remember that Emphyteusis is not a disease, nor Stillicide a crime. But though I would not willingly part with such scraps of science, I do not set the same store by them as by certain other odds and ends that I came by in the open street while I was playing truant.' The University was important for Louis less for the education it gave him than for the friends he made there, the wide reading he engaged in in the ample leisure that his casual attitude to his formal studies left him, the strengthening of his determination to become a writer encouraged by this reading, and the cultivation of a bohemian attitude and behaviour that were bound up with a growing revolt against Edinburgh gentility and all that it stood for. That revolt eventually turned against his father's religion, too, and precipitated a desperate crisis with his parents.

One aspect of his training as a lighthouse engineer which he enjoyed was his visits of inspection to Scottish lights and harbours. His grandfather Robert Stevenson had accompanied Walter Scott in 1814 on a voyage to inspect the lighthouses around the Scottish coast and select sites for new ones, and there was thus literary precedent for such an activity. In July 1868 he was at Anstruther, Fife, watching the harbour works there and in September he was at Wick, first with his father and then left by himself. He found Wick bleak and windy: 'bare grey shores, grim grey houses, grim grey sea', he wrote to his mother, and he watched a storm destroy his father's harbour works. In his memoir of his father he refers to the destruction of Wick harbour as 'the chief

The stretch of coastline near Wick, Caithness, seen by Louis on his tour of Scottish lighthouses in 1868.

with a streak of green and purple seaweed and a roll of white foam about their feet. The lighthouse stands on the highest — 190 feet above the sea; and there is only an uninhabited reef called the Out Stack between it and the Faroe Islands. The sketch is a little like their appearance as we steamed up to them from the south West; but wanting the jagged outline and the ... to mestoring and the colouring.

We steamed round between the lighthouse and the Out Stack (A in picture), with a great long swell from the north-ward splashing about her bows; and let the boat go from a point whence the reefs looked somewhat thus.

Page from a letter written by Louis to his mother on 18 June 1869, while he was on a second tour of the lighthouses. The lower sketch is of North Uist lighthouse.

disaster' of Thomas's life. 'The sea proved too strong for man's arts; and after expedients hitherto unthought of, and on a scale hyper-cyclopean, the work must be deserted, and now stands a ruin in that bleak, God-forsaken bay, ten miles from John-o'-Groats.'

Louis's tours to see lighthouses and harbours fed his appetite for the kind of scenery which calls out for appropriate action: three weeks on the little island of Erraid, off Mull, in 1870, when it was quarry and base for the building of the Dubh Artach Rock Lighthouse, completed in 1872, were to yield fruit both in 'The Merry Men' and in *Kidnapped*, while the awareness of tides and currents and swells, of rocks and sandbars and headlands, that these journeys gave him, supplemented by the constant instruction and illustration provided by his father when they walked the shore together, is reflected again and again in his novels and stories, both in the two mentioned and in 'The Pavilion on the Links', as well of course as in *Treasure Island*, among others.

On a parental allowance of ten shillings a week the undergraduate Stevenson perambulated the streets and haunted the pubs of Edinburgh (notably Rutherford's, just across the way from the University) with the friends that he now made and of whom he felt more and more a desperate need. Late in 1874 he was to write to a lady for whom he felt for a long time much more than friendship that his 'desiderata' were good health, two to three hundred pounds a year, and 'O du lieber Gott, *friends*!' Often he would retire to Swanston either alone or with a friend and meditate or talk about life and letters on Pentland walks. Among his friends now were Sir Walter Simpson (with whom he went on a walking tour in the Black Forest in 1872 and who was also his companion on the journey described in *An Inland Voyage*), who had recently inherited the baronetcy conferred on his father for his discovery of the anaesthetic uses of chloroform; James Walter Ferrier, son of a distinguished Professor of Philosophy at St Andrews and grand-nephew of the novelist Susan Ferrier; and the most long-lasting friend of all, the future lawyer and Louis's lifelong legal and financial adviser, Charles Baxter.

In March 1869 Louis was elected to the Speculative Society, the famous 'Spec', a debating society (still in existence) that had its own premises at Edinburgh University, though it was not officially a university society. He came to love the weekly meetings of the Spec and the pub talk at Rutherford's during the interval and after the meeting was over: it was a proving ground of friendship as well as a forum for the exchange of ideas and of witty banter. The ideas were often iconoclastic and rebellious. Looking back on these years in 1878, he wrote in his essay 'Crabbed Age and Youth' (which was later included in *Virginibus Puerisque*): 'I am no more abashed at having been a red-hot Socialist with a panacea of my own than at having been a sucking infant.' But revolutionary politics was not really Louis's line; his attitude was always more of the moralist than the politician and his attack on bourgeois hypocrisies rarely had definable political implications. That attack led him not only into demonstrating his opposition to conventional respectabilities by deliberate bohemianism of dress and behaviour; it led him to question Christian theology and Christian institutions in the name of Christian morality (one of the essays he read before the Spec was entitled 'Two Questions on the Relations between Christ's Teaching and Modern Christianity') and to seek out the company of prostitutes and drop-outs in the 'howffs' of Lothian Road.

He was self-conscious about his attitudes and adventures, and wrote poems about them:

Sir Walter Simpson, the Athelred of Louis's essay 'Talk and Talkers'. He 'presents you with the spectacle of a sincere and somewhat slow nature thinking aloud. He is the most unready man I ever knew to shine in conversation'.

> *I walk the streets smoking my pipe*
> *And I love the dallying shop-girl*
> *That leans with rounded stern to look at the fashions;*
> *And I hate the bustling citizen,*
> *The eager and hurrying man of affairs I hate,*
> *Because he bears his intolerance writ on his face*
> *And every movement and word of him tells me how much he hates me.*
>
> *I love night in the city,*
> *The lighted streets and the swinging gait of harlots.*
> *I love cool pale morning,*
> *In the empty bye-streets,*
> *With only here and there a female figure,*
> *A slavey with lifted dress and a key in her hand,*
> *A girl or two at play in a corner of waste-land*
> *Tumbling and showing their legs and crying out to me loosely.*

23

Tobacco rather than drink was a symbol of liberation for him:

> O fine, religious, decent folk,
>   In Virtue's flaunting gold and scarlet,
> I sneer between two puffs of smoke –
>   Give me the publican and harlot.

This was more than pose. He really did seek out publicans and harlots, and later reproached himself for having cut off communication with a prostitute whose repeated letters he left unanswered so that they might cease. 'O God,' he wrote to his confidante Mrs Sitwell, 'a thing comes back to me that hurts the heart very much. For the first letter she had bought a piece of paper with a sort of coarse flower-arabesque at the top of it.' He did not really have the conscience to support such behaviour. One of his poems begins:

> I have left all upon the shameful field,
>   Honour and Hope, my God, and all but life; ...

His parents, though becoming increasingly aware of differences of view between Louis and themselves, had no idea of his programmatic fornications. They continued to entertain his friends at Heriot Row. It was at Heriot Row, too, that Mrs Fleeming Jenkin, wife of the Professor of Engineering at Edinburgh University, first met Louis when she was having tea with his mother and came home to enthuse to her husband over this 'young Heine with a Scottish accent'. The Jenkins were important people in the cultural life of Edinburgh; both were passionately interested in amateur theatricals, and Mrs Jenkin presided over a salon for people of theatrical, literary and musical interests. Professor Jenkin was a polymath of great charm and vivacity. He is the Cockshot of Louis's essay 'Talk and Talkers', 'possessed by a demoniac energy, welding the elements for his life, and bending ideas, as an athlete bends a horseshoe, with a visible and lively effort'. He was sufficiently older than Louis to be able to advise and reprove him – sometimes with sharpness – without arousing Louis's resentment, yet young enough to become a real friend rather than a father-figure. Louis not only attended the Jenkin salon and acted in the Jenkin amateur theatricals: he came under the influence of a wise scepticism that extended to Louis's bohemian exhibitionism. His friends of his own age encouraged his sometimes witty and sometimes histrionic nose-thumbing at bourgeois Edinburgh. Jenkin helped him to mature.

The arrival of Louis's cousin Bob (Robert Alan Mowbray Stevenson), three years his senior, from Cambridge in 1870 provided an attractive and brilliant companion whom (together with his sister Katharine) he had already known and liked in his childhood. Bob's main interest was in painting – he was to write books on Rubens, Velasquez and Raeburn and ended up as Professor of Fine Arts at Liverpool – but it was as a young man of soaring imagination and fascinating conversation with his own fresh and vivid view of *la vie de Bohème* that he most impressed Louis. They walked together, talked together, drank together, and together played practical jokes on the good citizens of Edinburgh, designed to shake them out of their complacent respectability. The practical joke was part of the Stevenson arsenal of anti-bourgeois

Louis, dressed in his costume for a part in a theatrical production at Edinburgh University. 'I am getting on with my rehearsals, but I find the part very hard.' (Letter from Louis to Mrs Sitwell, April 1875.)

Thomas Stevenson, by George Reid. 'To Thomas Stevenson, civil engineer, by whose devices the great sea lights in every quarter of the world now shine more brightly, this volume is in love and gratitude dedicated by his son the author.' (Dedication of *Familiar Studies of Men and Books*.)

ammunition. Charles Baxter was another practitioner, and long after their student days he and Louis would contrive to bewilder and upset respectable business men with carefully contrived fake correspondence in which each warned against the other, Louis writing under an assumed name and character, such as Byron McGuinness. Louis and Charles indulged in the game of assumed personae for its own sake, even when they were both grown and responsible men, and the letters they exchanged in the roles of Johnson or Johnstone (Louis) and Thomson (Charles), two Scots-speaking religious hypocrites, are hilarious: the climax is Johnstone's letter, supposedly sent from 'Toddy Vale, by Kilrummer' to Thomson on 7 December 1883, telling how he left the Kirk to join the Morrisonian sect after having been accused of being 'No Bony-Feed wi' the plate' (that is, of taking money from the church collection plate); it is in a splendidly racy vernacular Scots.

Meanwhile, a crisis between Louis and his father was gradually developing. In April 1871 Louis made it clear that he could not and would not go on with engineering, and eventually a compromise was reached whereby he agreed to study for the law, a genteel and esteemed profession in Edinburgh and one which many of the great writers of the eighteenth and early nineteenth centuries, including Sir Walter Scott, had practised. As a kind of farewell to his career as a potential lighthouse engineer he read before the Royal Scottish Society of Arts on 27 March 1871 a paper 'On a New Form of Intermittent Light for Lighthouses', prepared presumably with his father's help. The paper won the Society's silver medal, for reasons which are obscure to the modern reader. But if this pleased his father, other aspects of Louis's behaviour did not. What had begun as heated arguments during long walks together in city or country turned into something much more desperate after Thomas's discovery, on 31 January 1873, of the written constitution of a society, founded under Bob Stevenson's inspiration, known as the L.J.R. The initials stood for Liberty, Justice and Reverence. Members, in addition to the Stevenson cousins, included Baxter and Ferrier, and the Society met at a pub in Advocate's Close, 357 High Street, to engage in wittily irreverent discussion. The constitution opened with the words: 'Disregard everything our parents have taught us.' Thomas's discovery of this document provoked an interrogation of Louis by his father on questions of religious belief. Louis replied candidly, 'but,' he wrote to Baxter on 2 February, 'if I had foreseen the real hell of everything since, I think I should have lied as I have done so often before.' He was desperately sorry for his parents, who now considered him a 'horrible atheist' and went about 'both ill, both silent', but he did not see what he could do other than what he had done. And the thought of his father 'praying down continuous afflictions upon my head' was not easy to bear.

Thomas blamed Bob Stevenson for leading his son astray, and meeting him in the street accused him, as Louis put it, 'of having ruined his house and his son'. Bob replied that he did not know where Louis had found out that the Christian religion was not true, but it was not from him. 'And I think from that point the conversation went off into emotion and never touched shore again.' Louis tried to explain his ideas about the differences between morality and religious institutions and to persuade his father that he accepted the ideals of Christian morality while repudiating the Church and the behaviour of most people who called themselves Christians. But his parents were touched on a most sensitive spot, and the thought that their son was an infidel was beyond the reach of rational distinctions. 'O Lord, what a pleasant thing it is to have just *damned* the happiness of (probably) the only two people who care a damn about you in the world!' wrote Louis to Charles Baxter in despair. And again: 'Here is a good cross with a vengeance, and all rough with rusty nails that tear your fingers, only it is not I that have to carry it alone; I hold the light end, but the heavy burden falls on those two.'

Painful conversations between father and son continued, Thomas probing for what he considered signs of grace and not finding them. 'I have made all my life to suit you,' Louis reports him as saying after one of these conversations ' – I have worked for you and gone out of my way for you – and the end of it is that I find you in opposition to the Lord Jesus Christ. . . . I would ten times sooner see you lying in your grave than that you should be shaking the faith of other young men and bringing ruin on other houses as you have brought it upon this.' But it was the pathos rather than the anger that most touched Louis. 'I thought,' his father said, 'to have had some one to help me when I was old.'

We know something of Louis's state of mind during this prolonged crisis from his letters first to Baxter and then, at a somewhat later stage, to a beautiful and intelligent woman twelve years his senior whom he first met in the late summer of 1873 when on a visit to his Balfour cousin Maud, wife of the Rector of Cockfield, Suffolk. She was Mrs Sitwell, born Frances Jane Fetherston-haugh, married at seventeen to a clergyman who proved to be of 'unfortunate temperament and uncongenial habits' (he may have been an alcoholic) and from whom, with her small boy, she was now living apart. Louis met her when she was a guest at Cockfield Rectory, and fell in love with her beauty and brilliance. Her closest friend was the literary and art critic Sidney Colvin, whom she was able to marry only after her husband's death and (what did not happen till 1901, seven years after that event occurred) Colvin's acquiring a financial position sufficiently comfortable to enable him to support a wife. Meanwhile she supported herself by translating and reviewing and acting as secretary to the College for Men and Women, Queen's Square, London, and was adored by most of the men who knew her. We are reminded forcibly of the difference between Victorian *mores* and ours in considering the lot of Mrs Sitwell, unable under the laws as they then existed to divorce her husband and committed to a life of chastity for as long as her husband lived. (Of course George Eliot had not accepted a similar situation a decade earlier, but Mrs Sitwell was no George Eliot nor would her friends have wanted her to be.) To Louis she became a combination of mother-figure, goddess and sweetheart. He confided in her in long letters, poured out to her his hopes and fears and frustrations and despairs, and, when he was actually in her physical presence (which he was as often as he could be), talked to her with passion and on occasion had to be sweetly but firmly dissuaded from crossing the invisible but absolutely firm line between lovingly confessional talk and anything physically erotic. His letters to her are often love-letters, if of a rather special kind. When no letter came from her he was in despair. He called her his Madonna and for some years his emotional life revolved around her. Of course he knew Colvin's position with relation to his Madonna, and accepted it, as Colvin (who became Louis's lifelong friend) accepted Louis's worship of the lady he intended one day to marry. This trio of friends and more than friends seems almost unbelievable to us today; but it was real and it worked, and within it Louis found both a confidante whom he could lovingly idealize and a friend who could give him practical help in entering the world of letters.

Louis thought of escaping from the intolerable situation at home by going to Cambridge; and then, in November 1873, his father met the Lord Advocate in a train and he suggested that Louis should read for the English rather than the Scottish Bar, which meant going to London and entering one of the Inns of Court. 'The Lord Advocate's advice goes a long way in Scotland,' Louis wrote to Mrs Sitwell. 'It is a sort of special legal revelation.' So to London he went, to eat the prescribed dinners and take the prescribed examinations, but he was prevented from doing this by a complete physical collapse following a throat infection. Feverish and emaciated, Louis was examined by the distinguished physician Andrew Clark, who forbade further study, diagnosed the possibility of 'consumption' (though seeing no definite trace of it yet), ordered a fattening diet, and recommended a stay in a milder climate such as that of the French Riviera. Louis's parents hastened up to London from Edinburgh, to be told by Dr Clark that their son needed a holiday on the Riviera *by himself*. Perhaps the doctor had some inkling of Louis's psychological need to have a breathing spell away from his parents; he appears to have been told, perhaps by Colvin, of Louis's troubles at home. 'Clark is a trump,' Louis wrote to Mrs Sitwell. Shortly afterwards he was writing to her from Menton.

By this time Louis had developed his own programme as an apprentice writer. He read widely and experimented with a variety of styles in both prose and poetry. From childhood he had 'lived with words' and practised descriptive writing for its own sake, as he tells us in his essay 'A College Magazine' (included in *Memories and Portraits*), but as he grew older he recognized that this kind of activity set him 'no standard of achievement'. So he began a programme of imitation: 'Whenever I read a book or a passage that particularly pleased me, in which a thing was said or an effect rendered with propriety, in which there was either some conspicuous force or some happy distinction in the style, I must sit down at once and set myself to ape that quality. I was unsuccessful, and I knew it; and tried again, and was again unsuccessful and always unsuccessful; but at least in these vain bouts, I got some practice in rhythm, in harmony, in construction and the co-ordination of parts. I have thus played the sedulous ape to Hazlitt, to Lamb, to Wordsworth, to Sir Thomas Browne, to Defoe, to Hawthorne, to Montaigne, to Baudelaire and to Obermann. . . . That, like it or not, is the way to learn to write; whether I have profited or not, that is the way.' It was certainly Louis's way, and it has led some critics to believe that he was no more than a verbal craftsman with nothing to say whose books are mere flourishes of bodiless technique. But Louis was also a troubled moralist, an heir of the Covenanters, a

In this letter, written to Mrs Sitwell from Siron's Inn during the summer of 1875, Louis addresses her (fourth line) as his Madonna.

Chez Sion

Nous n'irons plus au bois, les
lauriers sont coupés; that thing has
rung in my ears ever since I saw your
madonna. I could not write for a thousand
reasons; and even now, write only in the
teeth of a positive reluctance, lest you
should think I had forgotten you: which
is not so.

I have had one grey curious inertias
and desires to sleep these last days:
yesterday I slept almost the whole
day; but I am all right again
now. I should like to sleep a great
deal; I do not like being awake
and averse from work, which is
a virtuous feeling.

Béranger still trails on
I cannot get my back into anything.

Birds chirrup, cocks crow,

wryly humourous observer of his fellow men, a passionate student of topo-graphy with a deep feeling for the relationship between place and action. And his reading included Thoreau and Whitman as well as Darwin and Herbert Spencer, and this gave him both disturbing new ideas and encoura-ging new ideals. Whitman was particularly important for him, and his dis-covery of him marked an important moment in his student life. 'I date my new departure from three circumstances:' he wrote, looking back in 1880, 'natural growth, the coming of friends, and the study of Walt Whitman.' Among some notes left among these fragments of autobiography we find him associating his reading of Whitman and the coming of Bob Stevenson with a new direction in his ideas: 'Whitman: humanity: L.J.R.: love of mankind: sense of inequality: justification of art: decline of religion: I take to the New Testament: change startling: growing desire for truth: Spencer: should have done better with the New Test.'

Thus the young man who played the sedulous ape to earlier writers, and who joined with Bob Stevenson and Charles Baxter in activities designed to *épater les bourgeois* (including the practice of what they called 'Jink', defined as 'doing the most absurd acts for the sake of their absurdity and the conse-quent laughter'), was also painfully working his way through a variety of disturbing ideas towards a position from which he could view his fellow men. He never reached an assured position where he could rest contented as an observer of mankind with fixed moral standards; throughout his life, and increasingly as he grew older, he was aware of the moral ambiguities in human nature and of the difficulties of making absolute moral distinctions of which he nevertheless saw the necessity (for he was not an heir of the Covenanters for nothing); and he came to maturity as a writer when he was able to bring his various gifts and interests and doubts together and find a way of telling a story that was an 'objective correlative' of his troubled vision.

At the University Louis was one of the founders and editors of *Edinburgh University Magazine*, which survived for four numbers (January to April, 1871), and here he tried his hand at essay-writing. His essays at this time were studied pieces, each paragraph ending in a carefully contrived cadence. One of them, 'An Old Scotch Gardener', was later included, with some altera-tions, in his book of essays (all valuable to the biographer) entitled *Memories and Portraits* (1887). Others, such as 'The Philosophy of Umbrellas' and 'The Philosophy of Nomenclature', are rather coyly humorous pieces with distinct echoes of Charles Lamb, full of a bright self-consciousness. His first essay to be published in a regular periodical was 'Roads', written at Heriot Row in September 1873, rejected by *The Saturday Review* and accepted by *The Portfolio* where it appeared in the November issue. It is a very carefully worked out mixture of description and meditation, somewhat affected in diction ('A man must have thought much over scenery before he begins fully to enjoy it. It is no youngling enthusiasm on hill-tops that can possess itself of the last essence of beauty'), but with real adroitness in moving from long descriptive sentences to crisp generalizations about life and morality. The aesthete and the moralist are already seen here working together. His next published essay, 'Ordered South', was the direct result of his being sent to

Menton for his health, and we can trace its germination through the frequent letters he wrote to Mrs Sitwell during his stay there. It is the only essay in which Louis parades his invalidism: in all his other writing he compensates for his frequent illnesses by adopting a strenuously outdoor attitude or at least suggesting an authorial *persona* quite devoid of any physical disabilities. 'Ordered South' appeared in *Macmillan's Magazine* in May 1874, and was reprinted in *Virginibus Puerisque* (1881). Here he skilfully mingles descriptions of France and the Mediterranean with recollection of Edinburgh, and relates both to a brooding illumination of the ups and downs of an invalid's state of mind:

He is homesick for the hale rough weather; for the tracery of the frost upon his window-panes at morning, the reluctant descent of the first flakes, and the white roofs relieved against the sombre sky. And yet the stuff of which these yearnings are

Menton.

made, is of the flimsiest: if but the thermometer fall a little below its ordinary Mediterranean level, or a wind come down from the snow-clad Alps behind, the spirit of his fancies changes upon the instant, and many a doleful vignette of the grim wintry streets at home returns to him, and begins to haunt his memory. The hopeless, huddled attitude of tramps in doorways; the flinching gait of barefoot children on the icy pavement; the sheen of the rainy streets towards afternoon; the meagre anatomy of the poor defined by the clinging of wet garments; the high canorous note of the Northeaster on days when the very houses seem to stiffen with cold; these, and such as these, crowd back upon him. . . .

The essay gives a vivid picture of the moods of depression into which the sick man falls. 'He will pray for Medea: when she comes, let her either rejuvenate or slay.' He had written to Mrs Sitwell one Friday in November 1873: 'If you knew how old I felt! I am sure this is what age brings with it – this carelessness, this disenchantment, this continual bodily weariness. I am a man of seventy: O Medea, kill me, or make me young again!' His essays at this time move in the uncertain ground between self-expression and preciosity.

Louis's physical collapse had saved him from any further immediate conflict with his father. But when he felt himself restored by the Mediterranean sunshine he wrote at length to his father setting out his ideas on morality and religion, though fearful that this would lead to a complete break. But Thomas telegraphed back: 'Quite satisfied with your letter – keep your mind easy.' In fact, as Louis learned later, his parents were fearful for his sanity and were therefore determined to humour him at all costs. The immediate result, however, was to ease the situation, though this did not prevent Louis from worrying about his dependence on his father's money. Nearly ten years later, in 'Lay Morals', he described his dilemma at this time, in the person of 'a friend of mine; a young man like others; generous, flighty, as variable as youth itself, but always with some high motions and on the search for higher thoughts of life'. This young man, meeting at the University those 'who followed the plough in summer-time to pay their college fees in winter', felt guilty at his being 'unjustly favoured'. By what justice, he asked himself, could he spend money which 'belonged to his father, who had worked, and thought, and given up his liberty to earn it'. When he was sent abroad for his health his perplexities increased:

When he thought of all the other young men of singular promise, upright, good, the prop of families, who must remain at home to die, and with all their possibilities be lost to life and mankind; and how he, by one more unmerited favour, was chosen out from all these others to survive; he felt as if there were no life, no labour, no devotion of soul and body, that could repay and justify these partialities. . . . Like many invalids, he supposed that he would die. Now should he die, he saw no means of repaying this huge loan which by the hands of his father, mankind had advanced him for his sickness. In that case it would be lost money. So he determined that the advance should be as small as possible; and, so long as he continued to doubt his recovery, lived in an upper room, and grudged himself all but necessaries. But so soon as he began to perceive a change for the better, he felt justified in spending more freely, to speed and brighten his return to health, and trusted in the future to lend a help to mankind, as mankind, out of its treasury, had lent a help to him.

Colvin came out to visit Louis during part of the Christmas vacation, and found him 'without tangible disease, but very weak and ailing'. On 4 January Louis wrote to his mother that the two of them had moved from the Hôtel du Pavillon to the Hôtel Mirabeau, where the rooms were cheery and bright and the food was superb. He spent the winter at the Mirabeau, steadily improving in health and in his command of colloquial French and making some interesting friends. Notable among these were two Russian ladies, sisters, Mme Zassetsky and Mme Garschine, each with a child, whose frank talk and affectionately teasing manner with the young man, towards whom they cultivated a half-maternal, half-coquettish relationship, both bewildered and enchanted him. He was delighted with their two children, the younger of whom, 'a little polyglot button of a three-year-old', kept him continuously entertained. There was also Marie, daughter of an American couple, who, he wrote to his mother, 'is grace itself, and comes leaping and dancing simply like a wave'. He used his observation of the three little girls in writing his essay, 'Notes on the Movements of Young Children', published in *The Portfolio*, August 1874. Meanwhile, he wrote cheerfully to his mother and, at great length in a variety of moods, to Mrs Sitwell. He wrote to the latter that he was planning a book to be entitled *Four Great Scotsmen*, on John Knox, David Hume, Robert Burns and Walter Scott. (In the end he wrote essays only on Knox and Burns.) The Knox material was to be really new; Hume he had still to learn more about; 'Burns, the sentimental side that there is in most Scotsmen, his poor troubled existence, how far his poems were his personally, and how far national, the question of the framework of society in Scotland, and its fatal effect upon the finest natures. Scott again, the ever delightful man, sane, courageous, admirable; the birth of Romance, in a dawn that was a sunset; snobbery, conservatism, the wrong thread in History, and notably in that of his own land.' He was reading, among other things, Scottish history, and thinking seriously about problems of Scottish character and society. This reading and thinking were to bear important fruit in *Kidnapped, The Master of Ballantrae* and *Weir of Hermiston*.

Sidney Colvin in old age. 'You know best what you have done for me, and so you will know best how heartily I mean this.' (Letter from Louis to Colvin, on wishing him 'a very good year, free from all misunderstanding and bereavement', 1 January 1878.)

At the end of April Louis returned to Scotland, spending some time in Paris on his way north; in May we find him writing to Mrs Sitwell from Swanston: 'I have made an arrangement with my people: I am to have £84 a year – I only asked for £80 on mature reflection – and as I shall soon make a good bit by my pen, I shall be very comfortable. We are all as jolly as can be together, so that is a great thing gained.' His relations with his father were calm. He would continue with his law studies in Edinburgh, and at the same time try to place essays in periodicals. He had just finished an essay on Victor Hugo, he told Mrs Sitwell, and was looking around for another subject. 'I have been reading Roman Law and Calvin this morning.' Some days later he wrote her that he had 'received such a nice long letter (four sides) from Leslie Stephen about my Victor Hugo. It is accepted.' 'Victor Hugo's Romances' duly appeared in the August issue of *The Cornhill Magazine* and was reprinted in *Familiar Studies of Men and Books* (1882). He was also reviewing for *The Fortnightly Review* and *The Academy*. But it was a slender output: in the whole of 1874 he published only nine essays and reviews.

Louis in barrister's robes, 1875.

In June Louis was in London, with Colvin, and was elected to the Savile Club. He also saw his Madonna (whom at this time he was also calling 'Consuelo') and apparently professed his love in too ardent or too suggestive a manner, for later he wrote to her of his shame and his selfishness and acknowledged that she was to remain as 'the *Sun* . . . that is to shine on all, do good to all, encourage and support all'. He made important literary friends at the Savile, which from now on became his London centre. But Leslie Stephen was unable to arrange a meeting with Carlyle, whom Louis was most anxious to meet, finding him in a black and irritable mood. In August Louis went on a yachting trip on the west coast of Scotland with Sir Walter Simpson. He wrote to Mrs Sitwell from Oban expressing confidence in his health and his state of mind. 'I work like a common sailor when it is needful, in rain and wind, without hurt, and my heart is quite stout now.' He would be a man yet, he assured her, though he saw clearly in how much he was 'still selfish and peevish and a spoiled child'. He was trying desperately to turn

Mrs Sitwell into a pure mother-figure now, the 'mother of my soul' as distinct from the real 'mother of my body', and he sent her filial epistolary kisses. (Stephen Dedalus, in Joyce's *Ulysses*, distinguished his 'consubstantial' from his 'transubstantial' father; but that was thirty years later and the motive was very different: between the young bohemian Stephen and the young bohemian Louis a whole chapter in the history of the artist as exile and rebel had run its course.)

He went on with his law studies in Edinburgh (having given up the plan to read for the English Bar), and on 16 July 1875 he was admitted to the Scottish Bar. 'Accept my hearty thanks on being done with it,' wrote Fleeming Jenkin. 'I believe that is the view you like to take of the beginning you have just made.' It was indeed. Though a brass plate reading R.L. STEVENSON, ADVOCATE now appeared on the door of 17 Heriot Row, and he made a few perfunctory attempts to practise later in the year, Louis regarded the completion of his law studies simply as the fulfilment of a bargain he had made with his father, which would release him into the full freedom of the literary life. A few days later he was off to London and then to France.

Meanwhile, Louis had made a friend who was to play a very important part in his subsequent life. In February Leslie Stephen, who had come to Edinburgh to deliver a lecture, took him to visit W.E. Henley at the Edinburgh Royal Infirmary. Henley, poet, playwright, critic and journalist of a peculiarly robust temperament (known today largely for two poems, 'Invictus', beginning 'Out of the night that covers me', and the poem with the refrain 'I was a King in Babylon / And you were a Christian slave'), had already lost one foot as a result of tuberculosis of the bone and had come to Edinburgh to be treated by Joseph Lister in order to save the other: he bore the painful regular scrapings of the bone with great stoicism, and the foot was in fact saved. When Louis first met him he had already endured eighteen months of this treatment. 'It was very sad to see him there,' he wrote to Mrs Sitwell, 'in a little room with two beds, and a couple of sick children in the other bed; a girl came in to visit the children, and played dominoes on the counterpane with them; the gas flared and crackled, the fire burned in a dull economical way; Stephen and I sat on a couple of chairs, and the poor fellow sat up in his bed with his hair and beard all tangled, and talked as cheerfully as if he had been in a King's palace, or the great King's palace of the blue air. He has taught himself two languages since he has been lying there. I shall try to be of use to him.' The two men took to each other at once; a frank and vigorous friendship blazed up, to end in a famous quarrel and subsequent coldness that, as we shall see, was to have effects extending beyond Louis's lifetime.

He continued with essay-writing and reviewing. An article on Burns commissioned by the *Encyclopedia Britannica* was rejected as being 'too frankly critical, and too little in accordance with Scotch tradition', though the material was worked up later, without any change of attitude, in 'Some Aspects of Robert Burns', which appeared in *The Cornhill Magazine* in October 1879 and was reprinted in *Familiar Studies*. An article on Béranger for the *Britannica* was accepted. His essay on 'John Knox and his Relations to Women' – a really original and well-informed treatment of an aspect of Knox that had not been much discussed before – appeared in *Macmillan's Magazine* in September 1875 (it was also reprinted in *Familiar Studies*). He was travelling as much as writing, engaging in walking tours in Scotland, visiting Colvin in Cambridge, frequenting the Savile Club in London, visiting (in the spring of 1875) art colonies of France with his cousin Bob, travelling in Germany with his parents. He now saw himself as a lifetime wanderer, a sort of literary tramp: this was his version of the artist as exile. But if he felt the need to keep moving, he also had the late nineteenth-century artist's obliga-tory feeling of devotion to France as representing the true bohemian environ-ment for the free pursuit of a creative talent. Bob spent summers painting at Fontainebleau, and it was through Bob that Louis got to know this haunt of artists, epigoni of the 'Barbizon School' and their disciples who formed the kind of society that this young rebel writer found so congenial. Some period of every year from 1874 to 1879 Louis spent in this part of France, growing to know and to love the forest of Fontainebleau and the valley of the Loing. Barbizon, where Millet had lived, was a favourite place, and the inn there, Siron's, frequented by artists of all nations, had a special attraction for him. Looking back in 1884, in his essay 'Fontainebleau', he remembered it:

I was for some time a consistent Barbizonian; *et ego in Arcadia vixi*, it was a pleasant season; and that noiseless hamlet lying close among the borders of the wood is for me, as for so many others, a green spot in memory. The great Millet was just dead, the green shutters of his modest house were closed; his daughters were in mourning. The date of my first visit was thus an epoch in the history of art: in a lesser way, it was an epoch in the history of the Latin Quarter. . . .
  Siron's inn, that excellent artists' barrack, was managed upon easy principles. At any hour of the night, when you returned from wandering in the forest, you went to the billiard-room and helped yourself to liquors, or descended to the cellar and returned laden with beer or wine. The Sirons were all locked in slumber; there was none to check your inroads; only at the week's end a computation was made, the gross sum was divided, and a varying share set down to every lodger's name under the rubric: *estrats*. . . . At any hour of the morning, again, you could get your coffee or cold milk, and set forth into the forest. The doves had perhaps wakened you, fluttering into your chamber; and on the threshold of the inn you were met by the aroma of the forest. Close by were the great aisles, the mossy boulders, the intermin-able field of forest shadow. There you were free to dream and wander. And at noon, and again at six o'clock, a good meal awaited you on Siron's table. The whole of your accommodation, set aside that varying item of the *estrats*, cost you five francs a day; your bill was never offered you until you asked it; and if you were out of luck's way, you might depart for where you pleased and leave it pending.

  It was a good life, dining and talking with artists, wandering in the forest, planning essays and stories. Cheap though Siron's was, Louis could not have afforded it, or the life it symbolized, without money from his father, who presented him with £1,000 on his being admitted to the Bar. 'I fall always on my feet;' he wrote in May 1885, 'but I am constrained to add that the best part of my legs seems to be my father.' He was not even beginning to earn a living

Siron's Inn, Barbizon, in winter: a
photograph taken during the 1870s.
(*Left*) Street in Fontainebleau: an
illustration from Louis's essay,
'Fontainebleau', published in the
Magazine of Art, 1884.

from his writing: eight essays published in periodicals in 1876, five essays and stories in 1877, before his first book, a slim volume of travel, appeared in 1878, could not be expected to yield enough to support a man.

His periods in France stimulated an interest in fifteenth-century French history and literature, which bore fruit in his essays on Charles of Orléans (*Cornhill*, December 1876: reprinted in *Familiar Studies*) and François Villon (*Cornhill*, August 1877: similarly reprinted) and his stories 'A Lodging for the Night: A Story of Francis Villon' (*Temple Bar*, October 1877) and 'The Sire de Malétroit's Door' (*Cornhill*, January 1878). Throughout this period he was also working on essays later collected in 1881 as *Virginibus Puerisque*; some appeared in the *Cornhill* in June 1876; others appeared in *London* in 1878, and the last in the *Cornhill* again in 1879. These essays are the prime exhibits of the first phase of Stevenson's career as a professional writer: in a style which, while carefully mannered, no longer shows on the surface the influence of his models, he combines observations of the human and natural world, memories, moral apothegms and a wistfully earnest striving after generalizations about life; the hedonist and the puritan, the bohemian and the strenuous seeker after truth and values, alternate in a texture which seems sometimes charming, sometimes affected, sometimes pretentious. Later Louis was to learn to combine these conflicting aspects of his mind and

The bridge at Grez: oil-painting by Fanny Osbourne, *c.* 1875.

character into subtler ambiguities of plot and character in his fiction, and so became a writer worth full critical attention.

Louis's interest in Villon was associated with his interest in Robert Burns and in Burns's predecessor in eighteenth-century Scottish poetry, Robert Fergusson, who died at the age of twenty-four in the public bedlam of Edinburgh after (as Louis believed, but the facts are more complex than he realized) a life of dissipation. All three were both poets and rebels, both geniuses and moral defectives. Burns 'had trifled with life and must pay the penalty'; Fergusson was 'the poor, white-faced, drunken, vicious boy'; Villon, 'the sorriest figure on the rolls of fame', was 'a sinister dog, in all likelihood, but with a look in his eye, and the loose flexile mouth that goes with wit and an overweening sensual temperament'. Louis never wrote his planned essay on Fergusson, perhaps because he could never distance himself enough from the young Edinburgh roisterer with whom he felt a sympathy which amounted at times to identification. It is significant that Louis's fellow feeling for these three unrespectable poets co-existed with an unsparing moral judgment of them. Again we see the bohemian and the Covenanter inhabiting the same personality.

When he was not abroad, Louis lived at home in Edinburgh. His father, who was himself having strange moods of depression alternating with elation, no longer tried to probe his moral and religious beliefs, and a reasonable *modus vivendi* was achieved. A letter to Charles Baxter in February 1876, beginning 'My mother will be obliged if you will dine here on Wednesday at seven', indicates that Louis's friends were received socially at Heriot Row as a matter of course. But a letter to Baxter written in early July 1877, when he heard of his friend's imminent wedding, shows that he had not forgotten the threat of parental anger – and it shows, too, how he remained haunted by his bohemian days in Edinburgh even when he was growing out of that phase of his career:

If you have as good a time in the future as you had in the past, you will do well. For making all allowances for little rubs and hitches, the past looks very delightful to me: the past when you were not going to be married, and I was not trying to write a novel; the past when you went through to B[ridge] of Allan to contemplate Mrs Chawles in the house of God, and I went home trembling every day lest Heaven should open and the thunderbolt of parental anger light upon my head; the past where we have been drunk and sober, and sat outside of grocers' shops on fine dark nights, and wrangled in the Speculative, and heard mysterious whistling in Waterloo Place, and met missionaries from Aberdeen; generally, the past. But the future is a fine thing also, in its way; and what's more, it's all we have to come and go upon. . . .

Almost exactly a year before writing this letter Louis had arrived at Barbizon and learned from Bob, who was at nearby Grez, of a transatlantic female intrusion on the artists' group at the Grez *pension*. Louis followed Bob to Grez to investigate the situation and if necessary rescue his cousin from any entanglement with respectable American females. There were two of them, the thirty-seven-year-old Mrs Fanny Van de Grift Osbourne and her pretty seventeen-year-old daughter Isobel (Belle). It was Louis, not Bob, who became entangled, and Mrs Osbourne eventually became his wife.

Samuel C. Osbourne.

Frances Matilda Van de Grift (originally Vandegrift) was born in Indiana in March 1840 of Swedish and Dutch colonial stocks. Her father dealt in lumber and real estate. The Indiana of her childhood was a raw, developing state and she learned early to be enterprising and enduring. In December 1857 she married twenty-one-year-old Samuel C. Osbourne, then secretary to the Governor of Indiana, a man who combined considerable charm with complete instability of character. After a spell in the army during the Civil War he engaged in a variety of activities in a variety of places. He took to silver-mining and settled with his wife and baby daughter in Virginia City, where Fanny coped successfully with a very rough life indeed. But she could not cope with Sam, who disappeared to engage in further prospecting, leaving Fanny and little Belle to await him in San Francisco. Some time after he was presumed dead, he turned up at San Francisco to rejoin his family. A son, Samuel Lloyd Osbourne, was born in 1868. Sam obtained a comfortable job as a law-court stenographer and the family seemed to be settling down. But, though they now had a decent income and a decent house across San Francisco Bay in what is now East Oakland, Sam's behaviour continued to disturb his wife. She took the children and returned to her parents for a while, then came back for a final attempt to make the marriage work. She now acquired literary and artistic interests and made friends with San Francisco painters, musicians and literary men. She even, with her young daughter, attended an art school, and she won a silver medal for drawing. San Francisco at this time was anxious to establish itself as a cultural centre and encouraged a rather homespun interest in the arts. Fanny took part with gusto in the city's unsophisticated artistic activities; what she lacked in subtlety she made up for in energy. A second son, Hervey, was born. But Sam's infidelities and instabilities did not diminish, and in 1875 Fanny left him once more. This time she crossed the Atlantic, taking her children and a governess, to study art first in Antwerp and then in Paris. Sam seemed quite happy with the arrangement and apparently subsidized his wife during her absence.

The illness and death of little Hervey under particularly painful circumstances brought Sam from America, but he stayed only for a few weeks, and returned to America alone. While he was with his family they stayed at Grez to give Fanny a chance to recover from her ordeal, and on his departure Fanny, Belle, Lloyd and the governess returned to Grez. Fanny liked the scenery, the artistic atmosphere and the people. She liked especially Bob Stevenson, who was a more immediately appealing character than his cousin. But she got on well with the whole colony: both she and Belle were much admired and they were never without company. Louis was not yet involved. He was back in Scotland soon after first meeting Fanny, and returned to the Continent in August for the canoe trip with Sir Walter Simpson that he described in *An Inland Voyage*, his first book. That October Fanny was in Paris, and Bob visited her there, bringing Louis. Louis was now struck with her, calling her 'a very beautiful woman indeed' in a letter to his mother. They saw more and more of each other. She was at Grez again in the summer of 1877, and Louis spent the early part of that summer there, too, returning to Edinburgh for the latter part. But he was back in France in September, and

Fanny Osbourne: a photograph
taken at about the time she met
Louis.

Trusty, dusky, vivid, true,
With eyes of gold and bramble-dew,
Steel-true and blade-straight,
The great artificer
Made my mate.
          (From the poem 'My Wife')

This lithograph of Virginia City
was made in 1861, about the time
when Samuel Osbourne abandoned
Fanny there.

this time he had his post addressed to Fanny's new lodgings in Paris. In the spring of the following year Louis was writing to Henley: 'And do I not love? and am I not loved? and have I not friends who are the pride of my heart? O, no, I'll have none of your blues; I'll be lonely, dead lonely, for I can't help it; and I'll hate to go to bed where there is no dear head on the pillow, for I can't help that either, God help me; . . .' Louis and Fanny had been sleeping together in Paris, and neither seemed reluctant to let his friends know of their relationship.

Louis had been struck by what he described to a correspondent in 1882 as 'that love which may befall any of us at the shortest notice and overthrow the most settled habits and opinions'. He contemplated marriage, and the prospect sobered him: we can see how his mind was working in the second essay of *Virginibus Puerisque*: 'Times are changed with him who marries; there are no more by-path meadows, where you may innocently linger, but the road lies long and straight and dusty to the grave. Idleness which is often becoming and even wise in the bachelor, begins to wear a different aspect when you have a wife to support. . . . You have wilfully introduced a witness into your life, . . . and can no longer close the mind's eye upon uncomely passages, but must stand up straight and put a name to your actions.' He concludes, with characteristic wry self-mockery: 'To marry is to domesticate the Recording Angel. Once you are married, there is nothing left for you, not even suicide, but to be good.'

Of course, marriage would have to wait until after Fanny had got a divorce (easier for her in America than for Mrs Sitwell in England), but meanwhile there was the formidable problem of reconciling Louis's parents to his eventually marrying an American divorcee more than ten years older than himself. Both Mrs Sitwell and Colvin were called in to mediate with Thomas Stevenson, who had a soft spot for the former and would be likely to believe her testimony to Fanny's good character. Thomas actually went to Paris in February 1878 at Louis's request to discuss matters, but it is doubtful whether he met Fanny there or whether he learned that Louis contemplated eventual marriage to her. He was treating his son with kid gloves now, probably still nervous about his mental state, and Louis in his turn was trying to be honest with his father on moral and religious questions. 'I have taken a step towards more intimate relations with you,' he concluded a letter, written in Paris after his father had left, in which he defined his view of Christianity as 'a very wise, noble, and strange doctrine of life', but repudiated its other-worldly interests. '. . . This is a rare moment, and I have profited by it; but take it as a rare moment. Usually I hate to speak of what I really feel, to that extent when I find myself *cornered*, I have a tendency to say the reverse.' Thomas probably thought that in time the whole thing would blow over. After all, the lady was still married to someone else, and she would have to go back across the Atlantic before she could untie that knot; and, with the Atlantic between Louis and her, passion, on his part at least, would surely subside. In the summer of 1878, after a period in London when Louis discussed with her and Bob Stevenson the stories he was to publish in *The New Arabian Nights* in 1882, Fanny returned to California, perhaps because Sam had cut off funds.

Frontispieces of the first editions of *An Inland Voyage* (*opposite*) and *Travels with a Donkey* (*left*). Both books were illustrated by Walter Crane.

Louis at twenty-six: etching after a drawing by Fanny.

We do not know how strongly she felt committed to Louis at this time, but Louis certainly felt fully committed to her.

In June 1878 Louis was in Paris acting as secretary to Fleeming Jenkin who was a juror at the International Exposition there. In September he undertook the walking tour with a donkey in the Cévennes that he described in *Travels with a Donkey*, published the next year. This was his third book: in December 1878 (but dated 1879) *Edinburgh: Picturesque Notes* had appeared, with etchings by A. Brunet-Debaines after drawings by Sam Bough and others. He needed whatever he could make from the sale of his books: his essay-writing (at a guinea a page) had not yet earned him as much as £50 a year, and the £1,000 he had received from his father in 1875 was rapidly dwindling to nothing, thanks to his generosity to his impecunious literary friends.

An Inland Voyage, published in May 1878, had received favourable reviews but little public attention. Its mannered, whimsical, confidential style of controlled discursiveness was admired by a few discerning critics for its craftsmanship, but an account of a journey undertaken in order that it might be artfully written about afterwards was bound to appeal only to a minority taste. The same can be said of *Travels with a Donkey*, which contains some set pieces that pleased Louis himself and digressions about life and love which, as he wrote to Bob, were 'mere protestations to F'. Critical praise of the former book surprised its author, as he wrote to his mother. 'And the effect it has produced in me is one of shame. If they liked that so much, I ought to have given them something better, that's all. And I shall try to do so.' Some months later he wrote to his mother again on the same subject: 'I read *Inland Voyage* the other day: what rubbish these reviewers did talk! It is not badly written, thin, mildly cheery, and strained.' He had no illusions about his own work.

Louis returned from his travels with a donkey in October 1878, and spent some time in London working with Henley on one of the innumerable drafts of a play they were writing together, *Deacon Brodie*, based on the life of the respectable Edinburgh cabinet-maker who at night became a nefarious burglar (a combination of opposites that never ceased to interest Stevenson and was to receive its most explicit treatment in 1885 in *Strange Case of Dr Jekyll and Mr Hyde*). The two men worked on the play again at Swanston the following January. In July Louis was writing to Edmund Gosse, the critic and scholar of whom he had now made a good friend, about the essay on Burns he was working on. 'I made a kind of chronological table of his various loves and lusts, and have been comparatively speechless ever since. I am sorry to say it, but there was something in him of the vulgar, bagman-like, professional seducer.' But he goes on to talk with unbounded admiration of 'The Twa Dogs' and the 'Address to the Unco Guid', of whose merits, he says, 'even a common Englishman may have a glimpse, as it were from Pisgah'. His English literary friends, however close he felt to them, often provoked in Louis the expression of a half-humorous anti-English Scottish-ness. He concludes his letter to Gosse:

'*English, The*: – a dull people, incapable of comprehending the Scottish tongue. Their history is so intimately connected with that of Scotland, that we must refer our readers to that heading. Their literature is principally the work of venal Scots.' Stevenson's *Handy Cyclopaedia*. Glescow: Blaikie & Bannock.

But when his essay on Burns appeared in the *Cornhill* in October the Scots were furious at what they considered the insults dealt out to their national bard while the English were more appreciative. Louis had been very fair to the poems, but devastating about the poet's life and character. The moral judg-ment was savage, not tempered by any deep understanding of the social and psychological tensions under which Burns lived, but the essay was a genuine

'Reunion House, No. 10 West Street, one minute's walk from Castle Garden; convenient to Castle Garden, the Steamboat Landings, California Steamers and Liverpool Ships; Board and Lodging per day 1 dollar, single meals 25 cents, lodging per night 25 cents; private rooms for families; no charge for storage or baggage; satisfaction guaranteed to all persons; Michael Mitchell, Proprietor.' (Quoted in *The Amateur Emigrant*.)

new reading of the facts and deserved to be taken seriously. Louis, however, was not in Scotland to receive the blows aimed at him by indignant patriots. In August he had received a cable from Fanny: we do not know what it said, perhaps that she was ill and unhappy. But it decided him to set out for America at once. He sailed on the *Devonia* from Greenock on 7 August 1879, under the name of Robert Stephenson, without telling his parents and against the advice of his friends at the Savile Club. Only Baxter and Henley were entrusted with his American address: c/o Joseph Strong in Monterey, California. (Strong was a San Franciscan artist used by Fanny as intermediary for correspondence with Louis which she wanted kept secret from her husband: he was later to marry Belle Osbourne.) When it was learned at Heriot Row that Louis had left in pursuit of his American love, there was horror and anguish. But Louis was on the high seas, travelling 'by the second cabin' for eight guineas amid emigrants from all over northern Europe.

The second cabin, 'a modified oasis in the very heart of the steerages', was primitive enough, and Louis described the discomforts, as well as the interests and the incidents, of the ten-day voyage in the first part of *The Amateur Emigrant*, an account of his journey from Scotland to California written under difficult conditions in a grimmer and less mannered style than his earlier essays; it was intended for publication in *The Athenaeum*, but his friends and his father were distressed by its realism, and it was withdrawn, to be published with excisions in 1895 and in its complete form not until 1966. He spent one night and a day in New York, in continuous heavy rain. The night was spent at a cheap lodging-house where, as he wrote to Henley, he 'did not close an eye, but sat on the floor in my trousers and scratched myself from ten to seven'. The next day, 19 August, he visited booksellers and publishers, but was unable to interest anyone in commissioning work. He called at a chemist to try and find a cure for the itchy sores that covered his body. That Monday evening he assembled with the massed passengers from four emigrant ships,

This illustration from an American newspaper of 1869 shows a typical scene at a station on the Union Pacific Railway at this period.

all of which had arrived that week-end, at the Ferry Depot to be ferried across the Hudson to Jersey City, where the long train trek across the continent started. The crowding and discomfort were appalling, and Louis's state of mind was not made any easier by his finding a letter in New York telling him that Fanny had 'inflammation of the brain'. He describes the journey in the second part of *The Amateur Emigrant*. In spite of exhaustion, illness and anxiety he was continuously able to observe both people and landscape, and to keep alive his curiosity and that characteristically questing moral sense of his. (In one of the most interesting parts of this section of *The Amateur Emigrant* Louis discusses Negroes and Chinese in America and expands to the larger question of racial intolerance on which he speaks with an enlightenment uncommon at the time.) He changed trains more than once before joining the true emigrant train at the Union Pacific Transfer Station near Council Bluffs, on the eastern bank of the Missouri.

Louis managed to do some writing in the cramped and uncomfortable conditions of the long journey. He wrote to Colvin and Henley, even managing to enclose a poem on the Susquehanna to the former, as well as sending him the manuscript of 'The Story of a Lie', his first attempt to express in fiction the conflict between father and son, published in 1882. To Henley he wrote, on 23 August while crossing Nebraska: 'It is a strange vicissitude from the Savile Club to this; I sleep with a man from Pennsylvania who has been in the States Navy, and mess with him and the Missouri bird already alluded to. We have a tin wash-bowl among four. I wear nothing but a shirt and a pair of trousers, and never button my shirt. . . . I wonder if this will be legible; my present station on the wagon roof, though airy compared to the cars, is both dirty and insecure. I can see the track straight before and straight behind me to the horizon. Peace of mind I enjoy with extreme serenity; I am doing right; I know no one will think so; and don't care. My body, however, is all to whistles; I don't eat; but, man, I can sleep.' Two days

later he was writing to Henley about 'what it is to be ill in an emigrant train'. 'I confess I am not jolly, but mighty calm, in my distresses. My illness is a subject of great mirth to some of my fellow travellers, but I smile rather sickly at their jests.' He wrote also to Baxter, reminding him of his promise to provide news of his parents and enclosing a letter for his father. In the early morning of 30 August the train pulled up on the Oakland side of San Francisco Bay. 'The day was breaking as we crossed the ferry; the fog was rising over the citied hills of San Francisco; the bay was perfect . . .; the air seemed to awaken, and began to sparkle; and suddenly . . . the city of San Francisco, and the bay of gold and corn, were lit from end to end with summer daylight.'

Monterey, California, in 1875.

His destination was, however, the quiet little coastal town of Monterey, still essentially Mexican, some 130 miles to the south, where Fanny had gone to recuperate. The Southern Pacific railroad took him as far as Salinas, whence he went by narrow-gauge railway to Monterey. Research has revealed that Louis's first act in Monterey was to buy himself a stiff drink. Then he went to Fanny. What happened between them at their reunion we do not know. But Fanny, who was now well again, primly and deviously wrote to her old San Francisco friend Timothy Rearden: 'I hear that my literary friend from Scotland has accepted an engagement to come to America and lecture; which I think great nonsense. . . . Later on if he works and lives he will get both fame and money.' At the moment there seemed little prospect of either.

Fanny, together with her two children and her sister Nellie (who was soon to marry Adolf Sanchez of Monterey), was staying with a Mexican lady. Belle later testified that her mother was happy on Louis's arrival. 'Maybe my mother saw in this contrast to my father the security from infidelity that had wrecked their marriage . . . I . . . had no hope that she would not marry this penniless foreigner.' Lloyd recalled that Louis 'looked ill even to my childish gaze; the brilliancy of his eyes emphasized the thinness and pallor of his face'.

47

The house in Monterey where Louis
stayed in 1879.

He was indeed ill, and utterly worn out by his journey. Further uncertainty
about Fanny's divorce depressed his spirits. 'My news is nil,' he wrote
Baxter on 9 September. 'I know nothing, I go out camping, that is all I
know. Today I leave, and shall likely be three weeks in camp. I shall send
you a letter with more guts than this, and now say good bye to you, having
had the itch and a broken heart.' But his next letter, written on 24 September,
was 'from an Angora goat ranch where I live with some frontiersmen, being
fallen sick out camping'. He had gone camping in the Santa Lucia Mountains in search of health, and he had fallen desperately ill. For two nights he
'lay out under a tree in a sort of stupor' until the frontiersmen found him and
took him to their ranch, where they looked after him until he recovered. He
then returned to Monterey, lodging with a French doctor called Heintz,
who treated him when he had a relapse. On 29 November he wrote to Baxter
(asking for the second time for £50: Baxter was in charge of his finances,
but this was a loan), describing himself as 'sick both at heart and in body'
but also talking confidently of the 'towers of work' he had done. He had
already sent Henley 'The Pavilion on the Links', describing it as a 'grand
carpentry story in nine chapters, and I should hesitate to say how many
tableaux': it is a powerful melodramatic tale set with a great deal of topographical particularity and exploitation of atmosphere on the Scottish east
coast. And he was working on *The Amateur Emigrant*. He had also started a
novel, which he never finished, called *A Vendetta in the West*.

Louis lived in Monterey until late in December, when he moved to San
Francisco to be near Fanny, who had returned to Oakland to settle affairs
with her husband. In spite of regular bouts of illness and of depression, his
months at Monterey were not unhappy. 'This is a lovely place, which I am
growing to love,' he wrote to Henley. If Henley could be magically trans-
ported to Monterey, he would be deposited 'at Sanchez's saloon, where we
take a drink; you are introduced to Bronson, the local editor . . .; to Adolpho

48

Sanchez, who is delightful. Meantime I go to the P.O. for my mail; thence we walk up Alvarado Street together . . .; I call at Handsell's for my paper; at length behold us installed in Simoneau's little whitewashed back-room, round a dirty tablecloth, with François the baker, perhaps an Italian fisherman, perhaps Augustin Dutra, and Simoneau himself'. Louis ate regularly at the French restaurant of Jules Simoneau, the cheery 'fifty-eight-year-old wreck of a good-hearted, dissipated, and once wealthy Nantais tradesman', who looked after Louis like a father and anxiously went round to see how he was whenever he found him absent from his usual table. Louis was poor, and steadily growing poorer, his strenuous writing not yet having brought in any returns. Simoneau and some of his regular diners clubbed together to provide two dollars a week to enable Crevole Bronson, editor of the local newspaper, to hire Louis as a part-time reporter (Louis never knew where the money came from).

In San Francisco Louis lodged with an Irish family called Carson, and soon became good friends with the motherly Mrs Carson and her children. On 26 December he wrote to Colvin that for four days he had 'spoken to no one but to my landlady or landlord and to restaurant waiters. This is not a gay way to pass Christmas, is it? and I must own the guts are a little knocked out of me.' Sam Osbourne then lost his job, and it looked as though the impoverished Louis would now have to be financially responsible for Fanny as well as himself. On 26 January 1880 he wrote to Baxter: 'I have to drop from a 50 cent to a 25 cent dinner; today begins my fall. That brings down my outlay in food and drink to 45 cents, or $1/10\frac{1}{2}$ per day.' He was very ill again in February, but well enough by the twenty-second to write to Baxter about it. His state of mind was not improved by the determination of Colvin, Gosse and Henley to get him out of his American adventure, 'if without Mrs S., so much the better; if with her, then as the best of a bad job', as Colvin wrote to Baxter. Perhaps as part of this policy, Colvin wrote scathingly to Louis about the first part of *The Amateur Emigrant*, which had been sent him, and Henley and Gosse supported this view. Louis then became desperately ill again: Mrs Carson's four-year-old son developed pneumonia and Louis, wrung with pity for the child's suffering, sat up for hours nursing him, with dangerous consequences for himself. For six weeks, as he wrote to Gosse on 16 April, 'it was a toss-up for life or death'. He has been, he says, 'on the verge of a galloping consumption, cold sweats, prostrating attacks of cough, sinking fits in which I lost the power of speech, fever, and all the ugliest circumstances of the disease; and I have cause to bless God, my wife that is to be, and one Dr Bamford (a name the Muse repels), that I have come out of all this, and got my feet once more upon a hilltop, with a fair prospect of life and some new desire of living'. (Though Louis himself diagnosed incipient 'consumption', and for the rest of his life he was regarded as either suffering from or continuously threatened by tuberculosis, it is worth recording that one modern medical expert who has thoroughly examined all the evidence is convinced that he never suffered from tuberculosis but from another chest disease, bronchiectasis, which often begins in childhood following pneumonia or whooping cough or repeated acute episodes of bronchitis. This

Married by me at my residence 19th May 1880
Robert Louise Stevenson born Edinboro', Scotland,
and   White single, 30 years old, resides
                in Oakland, Cal
Fannie Osbourne, born Indianapolis, Indiana,
witnesses   40 years, widowed, white, resid in
Dora N. Williams   Oakland
Anna Sara. Certificate to be sent to Mrs Virgil Williams

Record of the marriage of Louis and Fanny, written by the minister. Fanny is described as 'widowed'.

disease is characterized by persistent pulmonary haemorrhage and other symptoms from which Louis suffered intermittently all his adult life.) Fanny moved to a hotel in Oakland to watch over Louis in his illness and convalescence and then brought him to her own cottage, with Nellie as chaperone if one were needed in his condition. In spite of everything, he kept on writing whenever there was the barest physical possibility.

The financial situation was now desperate. He wrote to Baxter instructing him to sell his books. Perhaps as a result of this Baxter intervened with Louis's parents, or perhaps, as has been surmised, Fanny wrote to them surreptitiously about their son's health, but whatever the cause at the end of April they relented. 'My dear people telegraphed me in these words: "Count on 250 pounds annually,"' he wrote to Colvin triumphantly. Meanwhile, Fanny had got her divorce. On 19 May 1880 Louis and Fanny crossed the bay to San Francisco and were married there by a Scottish Presbyterian minister in his home. Louis was still far from well: indeed, both parties spoke of their union as 'a marriage *in extremis*'. Fanny's immediate task was to nurse her husband back to health. It was one with which she was to grow increasingly familiar in the course of their life together.

Fanny was determined to get Louis away from the fogs of San Francisco. At first it was planned that they should stay at a house near the head of the Napa valley owned by Virgil Williams, founder of the San Francisco School of Design, where Fanny had studied: he and his wife Dora were old friends of Fanny and now good friends of both her and Louis. When this plan came to nothing Louis and Fanny and young Lloyd Osbourne spent a short time in a cottage in the grounds of the Hot Springs Hotel at Calistoga (arranged by Sam Osbourne, who bore Fanny no malice and remained on good terms with the newly married couple) and then a longer period in a deserted cottage on the site of an abandoned gold and silver mine high above the Napa Valley on the south-eastern slope of Mount Saint Helena. Louis described the hardships, misadventures, excitements and enthusiasms of this primitive life, as well as the characters they became involved with and the scenery they were surrounded by, in *The Silverado Squatters*, part of which was first published in *The Century Illustrated Magazine* in November and December 1883 and all of which appeared immediately afterwards in book form with a frontispiece by Joe Strong (who visited them there) showing Louis and Fanny in their Silverado shack.

Louis and Fanny in their shack at Silverado: woodcut frontispiece of *The Silverado Squatters*, designed by Joe Strong.

50

John Addington Symonds, the Opalstein of Louis's essay 'Talk and Talkers'. 'His various and exotic knowledge, complete although unready sympathies, and fine, full, discriminative flow of language, fit him out to be the best of talkers; so perhaps he is with some, not *quite* with me – *proxime accessit*, I should say.'

By July Louis seemed well enough to contemplate returning to Scotland with his new wife. Fanny had initiated a correspondence with his parents, writing with great tact and charm, and they were now anxious to meet her. Louis himself (who had earlier written of his father to Colvin: 'Since I have gone away, I have found out for the first time how I love that man; he is dearer to me than all, except Fanny') was keen to cement the reconciliation with a personal appearance. So back they went, first to San Francisco and then – by Pullman this time, a great contrast to the emigrant train on which Louis had travelled westward – to Chicago and then New York. They sailed first class on 7 August 1880 on the *City of Chester*, which arrived at Liverpool on 17 August, a year and ten days since Louis had set out on the *Devonia*. His parents and Sidney Colvin were at Liverpool to meet him. Colvin, who was later to praise Fanny publicly as 'a character strong, interesting, and romantic almost as his [Louis's] own; an inseparable sharer of all his thoughts, and staunch companion of all his adventures; the most open-hearted of friends to all who loved him; . . . and in sickness, the most devoted and most efficient of nurses', privately expressed doubts as to whether Louis's old friends 'will ever get used to her little determined brown face and white teeth and grizzling (for that's what it is) grizzling hair'. In later years Fanny tried to protect Louis from many of his old male friends whose company she considered bad for his health (and perhaps his character, too), and they resented her as a result, but Colvin, for all his reservations, was determined to get on well with Fanny, and did so. As for Louis's parents, the reconciliation was warm and absolute. Fanny played her part superbly, charming Thomas by her liveliness and sturdy common sense and his wife by her obvious devotion to Louis and her clear assumption that Louis's wife and mother were partners in dedicated love of him. She in her turn was profoundly impressed by the upper-middle-class luxury of 17 Heriot Row. Everyone agreed that Fanny could manage Louis. 'I too married a besom and never regretted it,' his uncle George Balfour remarked approvingly. So they set off for a Highland holiday in Strathpeffer in high spirits. There Louis renewed his interest in Scottish history and topography.

But it soon became clear that Louis's love of Scotland was not reciprocated by that country, and that a Scottish winter might well be fatal to him. Uncle George (who was a doctor), alarmed at his nephew's emaciated condition and the state of his chest, advised a stay in the High Alps, which medical opinion then favoured as a good climate for consumptives. So by mid-October Louis and his new family (which now included, as well as Fanny and Lloyd, a Skye terrier and a Manx cat: the cat, which totally resisted house-training, had to be left in England) started on their travels again, and on 4 November reached Davos, the health resort in south-east Switzerland situated in the highest part of the Alpine valley of Davos, already popular with consumptives and later to be the scene of Thomas Mann's novel *The Magic Mountain*. There they stayed until April 1881.

En route for the Continent Louis had a bibulous lunch with his Savile Club friends and Fanny and Louis between them ran up a huge bill at the Grosvenor Hotel. It was now that Fanny's suspicion of Louis's friends –

'fiends disguised as friends' she called them in a hot outburst – as enemies of his health first began. They proceeded in leisurely fashion to Davos, stopping at Troyes and elsewhere on the way. Louis found Davos a rather dreary place, with its snow-covered mountains and long bleak valley, and life in their hotel there, surrounded by fellow invalids, was far from stimulating. But there were compensations. Louis got on well with twelve-year-old Lloyd, who hero-worshipped him. And he made friends with John Addington Symonds, the art historian, critic, minor poet and authority on the Italian Renaissance, who was also there for his health. Mrs Sitwell arrived with her dying son, and both Louis and Fanny helped where they could and admired the mother's fortitude. The boy's death, after he had lingered painfully, wrung from Louis one of his best-known poems, beginning

> *Yet, O stricken heart, remember, O remember*
> *How of human days he lived the better part.*
> *April came to bloom and never dim December*
> *Breathed its killing chills upon the head or heart.*

Two years later, when Charles Baxter lost a little daughter, the only comfort that Louis could give was again that the child would have no future suffering to encounter. He had a special feeling for children, but chose deliberately not to have any of his own, partly because of his always uncertain health and partly because he felt himself emotionally too vulnerable. After watching the agonies of the Carson child in San Francisco he had written to Colvin: 'O never, never any family for me! I am cured of that.'

Watercolour of Davos, painted in 1882–83, shortly after the Stevensons stayed there.

The cottage at Braemar, where the Stevensons stayed during August and September 1881. It was here that Louis began to write *Treasure Island*. It was known as 'the late Miss M'Gregor's cottage', but, as Louis wrote in a letter to Gosse, 'The reference to a deceased Highland lady (tending as it does to foster unavailing sorrow) may be with advantage omitted from the address, which would therefore run – The Cottage, Castleton of Braemar.'

Dr Karl Ruedi gave the prognosis that two years at Davos might well permanently arrest Louis's disease, but two years were more than Louis could face. He found no inspiration in the Davos environment, and though he planned a fair amount he wrote little. In December 1880 he wrote to his father about a book he planned to write on the history of the Highlands from the defeat of the Jacobite Rebellion of 1715 to the present time, and asked for relevant books. He wrote optimistically about living 'as much as possible in the Highlands' while completing this work and persuaded himself that it would be good for his health. On Boxing Day 1880 he wrote his mother a long letter about religion and morality, concluding that 'the whole necessary morality is kindness; and it should spring, of itself, from the one fundamental doctrine, Faith'. In January 1881 Colvin came out, and 'found him apparently little improved in health, and depressed'. In April Louis and Fanny (Lloyd was now at school in Bournemouth) left Davos, and after a nostalgic visit to Barbizon and a few days in Paris they arrived back in Scotland in late May, and, together with Louis's mother, rented a cottage in Pitlochry. The weather was not good. In August the party, now including Lloyd, moved further north to Braemar, but the summer stayed wet and chilly.

But in spite of bad weather and bouts of illness, Louis was now able to write again. The two months at Pitlochry had been productive: in them he wrote one of his finest short stories, 'Thrawn Janet' (published in the *Cornhill* in October 1881), and 'The Merry Men', which he called 'a fantastic sonata about the sea and wrecks' in an enthusiastic letter to Henley. It was published in the *Cornhill* in June and July 1882. 'It is, I fancy, my first real shoot at a story, an odd thing, sir, but, I believe, my own, though there is a little of Scott's *Pirate* in it, as how should there not be? He had the root of romance in such places.' It is indeed a powerful story of sea and storm and wrecks and guilt, but 'Thrawn Janet' is the more masterly tale. It shows the preoccupation with evil and in particular with the Devil which was one of the characteristics of Scottish Calvinism and thus part of Louis's religious inheritance: it is a grim tale of a Scottish minister and his diabolically possessed housekeeper set in an appropriately bleak Scottish landscape, 'the moorland parish of

Balweary, in the vale of Dule'. Surprisingly, Louis stressed the sensational rather than the psychologico-moral aspect of the story, and thought of it as the first of a planned series of 'crawlers', or horror stories, to which Fanny would also contribute. (Fanny was keen on 'crawlers' and seems to have influenced him here.) The series was never completed, though *The Merry Men and Other Tales and Fables*, published in 1885, includes both the title story and 'Thrawn Janet' as well as the later 'Markheim', another powerful story of moral ambiguities, of which the hero is a murderer with a complex conscience whom the Devil tempts to further crime and vice only to reveal himself in the end as a redemptive angel in disguise. The truth is that Louis's concern with 'crawlers' was a temporary over-simplification: he was not really interested in horror stories as such, but liked to use them as vehicles of moral and topographical exploration, as he was to do most successfully of all in *Dr Jekyll and Mr Hyde*.

It was also while he was at Pitlochry that Louis heard of the resignation of the Professor of History and Constitutional Law at Edinburgh University and thought it worth applying for the Chair himself. Its duties involved only some lecturing in the summer session, and the election was in the hands of the Faculty of Advocates, of which Louis was of course a member. He collected supporters, and was stimulated to plan further work on Scottish history to prove his fitness. He was too late in his application, but the incident is significant in that it led him to an exploration of an area of Scottish history which was to bear fruit in *Kidnapped*.

At Braemar they were visited by Colvin, Baxter and others, and by a Dr Alexander Hay Japp, authority on Thoreau, who wanted to discuss Louis's essay on Thoreau with him. Dr Japp discovered that, stimulated by a map of an imaginary island that Louis had drawn for Lloyd, Louis had embarked on an exciting boys' adventure story about pirates, and knowing the proprietor of the boys' magazine *Young Folks*, Japp arranged for it to be serialized there. Louis's first novel thus appeared in due course as a serial in a boys' magazine between October 1881 and January 1882. Inspired by Lloyd's excitement about the map, and encouraged by his father who was visiting them, Louis had set about inventing a story to fit the map. His father enthusiastically contributed various details. Chapters were read aloud to the family and to visitors as they were written. 'If this don't fetch the kids, why, they have gone rotten since my day,' he wrote to Henley. The first three chapters, he wrote, were 'heard by Lloyd, F., and my father and mother, with high approval. It's quite silly and horrid fun, and what I want is the *best* book about the Buccaneers that can be had.' He called it *The Sea-Cook*, but it appeared in *Young Folks* as *Treasure Island*, by 'Captain George North'. It was published as *Treasure Island* in book form in 1883. In inventing the story Louis drew on his childhood reading and imaginings, his and his father's lighthouse experiences, the scenery of the California coast, his characteristic desire to fit actions and characters to scenes to which he considered them appropriate, and – this is what makes the book so remarkable as an adventure story – his lifelong preoccupation with moral ambiguities. The moral complexities of the story, which do not interfere with its speed and interest as a splendid yarn, must have escaped its original readers, but the modern reader finds them arresting. The hero is really the villain, Long John Silver (based partly on Henley), and what is, superficially at least, admirable, is not always what is right. The immediate interest lies in the quest, not in the nature and significance of what is sought after. The quest is both a good thing and a symbol of the greed and selfishness of those who pursue it. And the boy narrator is both a spoiled 'lucky Jim' and an enviably daring youngster. The story moves along at a terrific pace; at each point the physical setting gives vividness and added meaning both to character and action. *Treasure Island*, in short, gave a new dimension to the adventure story.

Louis's achievement in transforming the cliché-ridden Victorian boys' adventure story into a classic of its kind was not immediately suspected even by himself. But his enthusiasm did lead him to write to Henley: 'I love writing boys' books. This first is only an experiment; wait till you see what I can make 'em with my hand in.' He waxed eloquent over 'Jerry Abershaw', highwayman hero of a planned but never written novel, and experimented with picturesque and arresting openings. It may have been the stimulation of childhood memories as a result of all this that led him at this time to write the first of those verses for children which later became *A Child's Garden of Verses*.

The summer was a poor one in Scotland in 1881, and when the weather grew even worse in September and Louis once again succumbed to severe respiratory illness it became clear that he would have to go south. By 18 October he and Fanny and Lloyd were at Davos again. This time they did not stay in a hotel but rented a chalet belonging to the Hôtel Buol, where they had more privacy and could more easily lead their own kind of life. Symonds was living in the Hôtel Buol. Louis was now in better form than during his previous stay in Davos. He played a variety of imaginative games with Lloyd. He wrote to his father for books about the Appin Murder, about which he proposed to write a book but which eventually became the mainspring in the plot of *Kidnapped*. He finished *Treasure Island* (as he had to, because it was already running as a serial) at the top of his form. He meditated a life of Hazlitt.

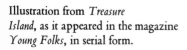

Illustration from *Treasure Island*, as it appeared in the magazine *Young Folks*, in serial form.

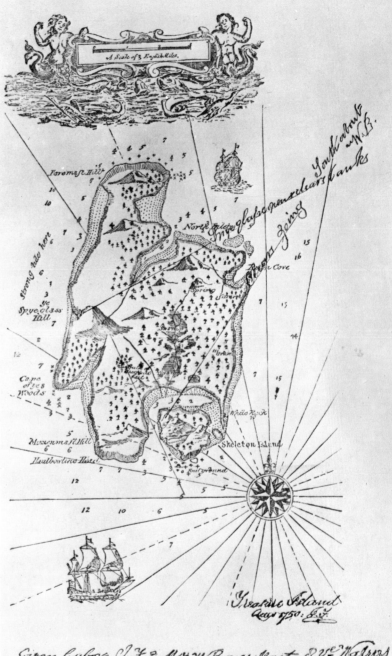

The frontispiece of the first edition of *Treasure Island*. The map is based on the original map which Louis drew while staying in Braemar.

(*Top*) Advertisement at the end of
Louis's book *Moral Emblems*, printed
at Davos in 1882 by Louis and
Lloyd on their own press. (*Below*)
'The Careful Angler': a woodcut
illustration, by Louis, from *Moral
Emblems*. 'I got a penny a cut and a
halfpenny a set of verses from the
flint-hearted publisher, and only one
specimen copy, as I'm a sinner.'
(Letter from Louis to Gosse, 23
March 1882.)

He amused himself by making wood-engravings for the printing-press that began as Lloyd's hobby and was now also his. And he wrote to Baxter asking for 'a little Edinburgh gossip, in heaven's name' and recalling with nostalgic relish the escapades of their student days. 'O for ten Edinburgh minutes, sixpence between us, and the ever glorious Lothian Road, or dear mysterious Leith Walk! . . . Do you remember Brash [a publican]? the L.J.R.? the sheet of glass that we followed along George Street? Granton? the night at Barrymuirhead? the compass near the sign of the Twinkling Eye? the night I lay on the pavement in misery?'

Fanny became ill in December and had to go to Berne for treatment: Louis brought her back to Davos on Christmas Day in an open sleigh – a seven hours' journey in freezing cold, but, as he wrote his mother, 'none of us a penny the worse'. He kept on writing. He completed *The Silverado Squatters* and got far into *Prince Otto*, the strangely coy Ruritanian romance that shows Louis's bohemianism, preciosity and moralism in artful but unsatisfactory combination: it was published in 1885. He produced essays, notably the two entitled 'Talk and Talkers' which appeared in the *Cornhill* in April and August 1882 and in *Memories and Portraits* in 1887. He gave up his projected life of Hazlitt after much reading: Hazlitt's *Liber Amoris* was too much for him. He prepared *Familar Studies of Men and Books* for the press: it included the critical essays he had written between 1875 and 1881, and appeared in 1882. He wrote 'A Gossip on Romance' (published in *Longman's Magazine* in November and then in *Memories and Portraits*), in which he defined, in deliberately over-simplified form, his topographical sense as a writer of stories. 'Some places speak distinctly. Certain dank gardens cry aloud for a murder; certain old houses demand to be haunted; certain coasts are set apart for shipwreck. . . . The old Hawes Inn at the Queen's Ferry makes a similar call upon my fancy. There it stands, apart from the town, beside the pier, in a climate of its own, half inland, half marine – in front, the ferry bubbling with the tide and the guardship swinging to her anchor; behind, the old garden with the trees. Americans seek it already for the sake of Lovel and Oldbuck, who dined there at the beginning of the *Antiquary*. But you need not tell me – that is not all; there is some story, unrecorded or not yet complete, which must express the meaning of that inn more fully.' He found that story eventually in an early chapter of *Kidnapped*. On 1 April 1882 Louis wrote to Dr Japp that his wicked carcass was holding together wonderfully. 'In addition to many other things, and a volume of travel, I find I have written, since December, 90 *Cornhill* pages of magazine work – essays and stories: 40,000 words, and I am none the worse – I am the better.' Later in April he wrote to Henley: 'My lungs are said to be in a splendid state. A cruel examination, an exa*nim*ation I may call it, had this brave result. *Taïaut*! Hillo! Hey! Stand by! Avast! Hurrah!'

They left Davos with no regrets, and were back in Edinburgh by 20 May. They then spent a fortnight at the manse of Stobo, Peeblesshire, where in spite of moods of gaiety (which produced a memorable letter to Henley about imaginary 'old Mr Pegfurth Bannatyne', supposedly staying at a country inn near by, and his recollections of Hazlitt and Wordsworth), he was again stricken by respiratory illness. He went to London to consult Dr Clark, who suggested Speyside. So the family went north and settled for a month at Kingussie – the last complete month Louis ever spent in Scotland. But again the weather was not good, and Louis suffered a haemorrhage. He returned to London early in September to seek Dr Clark's advice again. Dr Clark said that there was no need to return to Davos (a verdict which Louis and Fanny both heard with relief) but that they ought to seek a congenial southern climate. So off they went to the south of France, and found Campagne Defli, an attractive and spacious house in pleasant surroundings at St Marcel, a suburb of Marseilles. But something about the district disagreed with Louis, and he remained unwell and depressed while staying there. Then in December an outbreak of fever, which Fanny took to be typhus, broke out in the neigh-bourhood and she dispatched Louis at once to Nice, following herself, in a thoroughly alarmed state, after she had shut up the house. In the course of fleeing from fever and looking for a healthier place they found Hyères, a winter resort about ten miles east of Toulon on the Côte d'Azur. There they rented the Châlet La Solitude, which Colvin called 'a cramped but habitable cot-tage built in the Swiss manner, with a pleasant strip of garden, and a view and situation hardly to be bettered', but which Louis enthusiastically de-scribed to Mrs Sitwell as 'the loveliest house you ever saw, with a garden like a fairy story, and a view like a classical landscape. . . . Eden, madam, Eden and

Kingussie, Inverness – some of the last Scottish scenery which Louis saw.

Edmund Gosse, by Sargent.

Beulah and the Delectable Mountains and Eldorado and the Hesperidean Isles and Bimini.' This was their home until they were driven from it by an outbreak of cholera in the summer of 1884. And in spite of severe bouts of illness – including frequent haemorrhages, malaria and an eye infection that necessitated his keeping his eyes bandaged – and of personal anxieties and griefs, the latter occasioned notably by the death from alcoholism and tuberculosis of his dissipated old friend James Walter Ferrier, this was a happy time for Louis. 'I was only happy once,' he wrote to Colvin from Samoa many years later, 'that was at Hyères.'

At St Marcel and Hyères Louis worked at, among other things, his children's poems – poems not so much for children as about children, based on vividly recollected scenes in the life of the imaginative and frequently sick little boy of 17 Heriot Row. The desire for travel and adventure coupled with the reassurance of friendly domestic objects and routines shown in these poems reflects the same counterpointing of escape and excitement on the one hand and cosy fireside conviviality on the other that can be found in many of the novels and stories. The sense of the countryside as a map (seen from a tree-top or a swing), the response to different seasonal scenes, memories of Edinburgh's New Town, of Colinton Manse, of Edinburgh weather – we find these in the poems as we find them in so many of the novels. At their best they have a clarity of line, a precision of diction and an honesty of recollection and re-enactment that make them unique poems of their kind. Writing them was originally suggested by Kate Greenaway's *Birthday Book for Children*, but the all-pervasive autobiographical element marks an essential difference. The original title was *Penny Whistles*, but they were published, in a volume containing other poems of the same kind which he wrote after he left Hyères, as *A Child's Garden of Verses* in 1885. At Hyères Louis also did some more work on *Prince Otto* and began *The Black Arrow* for *Young Folks*. This adventure story set in the time of the Wars of the Roses was not much thought of either by himself or by his friends; but it has a grimness in its awareness of the realities of fifteenth-century life and warfare together with a refusal to arrange the moral pattern in the black-versus-white manner of most stories of this *genre* – once again, Louis's interest in moral ambiguities – which give it a certain distinction. *Treasure Island* was published in book form in November 1883, and rapidly proved to be his first real popular success. He was modestly content – indeed, delighted – to receive for it, as he wrote to his parents, 'a hundred jingling, tingling, golden, minted quid'. In September he wrote to Gosse that 'this year, for the first time, I shall pass £300' in money made from writing.

Friends came to visit. There was a visit to Nice with Henley and Baxter at the beginning of 1884 and Louis fell dangerously ill there. Fanny came and brought him back to Hyères: she was indignant with his friends and considered the junketings they encouraged him to indulge in as dangerous to his health and indeed to his life. She increased her watchfulness, forbidding convivial sessions and banishing from Louis's presence anyone who had a cold and might infect him: for his worst attacks often began with a simple cold. The doctors in Nice told Fanny there was no hope and advised her to send for a

60

This page from an early edition of *A Child's Garden of Verses* shows Louis's fascination, which began in childhood, with high places and distant views.

member of the family to be with her at the end. Bob Stevenson came. 'He helped me to nurse Louis, and he kept me from despair,' Fanny later testified. In May Louis developed eye trouble and was 'condemned to darkness, double green goggles and a shade,' as Fanny wrote Baxter. Early in May Louis suffered the most violent and dangerous haemorrhage he had so far experienced. He was unable to speak, and communicated with Fanny in writing. 'Don't be frightened; if this is death it is an easy one,' he wrote down for her when he lay choked with blood. Fanny, who had been in a desperate enough state in Nice, when the doctors confidently predicted that Louis would die, was now thrown into despair and 'sat and gloomed', but Louis teased her back to good humour by his notes. Thomas Stevenson was himself ill during Louis's illness and was unable to visit his son, but Henley and Baxter sent their doctor from London to examine Louis. On 18 May Louis's mother wrote: 'The doctor says, "Keep him alive till he is forty, and then although a winged bird he may live to ninety." But between now and forty he must live as though he were walking on eggs, and for the next two years, no matter how well he feels, he must live the life of an invalid.' Fanny took note, and acted accordingly. She has had her detractors, but the plain fact is that she kept Louis alive.

An illustration from the first edition of *The Black Arrow* (1888).

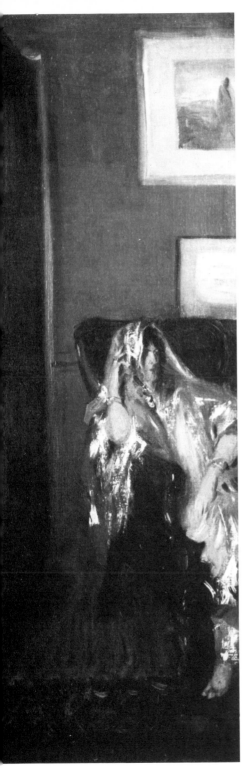

A painting by Sargent of Louis and
Fanny at 'Skerryvore', their house
(*above*) in Bournemouth. This, the
second of two portraits of Stevenson
painted by Sargent at Bournemouth,
was done in the summer of 1885.
'Sargent was down again and painted
a portrait of me walking about in my
own dining-room, in my own
velveteen jacket, and twisting as I go
my own moustache; at one corner a
glimpse of my wife, in an Indian
dress, and seated in a chair that was
once my grandfather's. . . . (Letter
from Louis to W. H. Low,
22 October 1885.)

Driven from Hyères by cholera in the early summer of 1884, the Stevensons settled on the south coast English resort of Bournemouth as one place in Britain where the climate would be tolerable for Louis. They lived there from September 1884 to August 1887. One motive in leaving the Continent was to be nearer Thomas, who had had a series of strokes and was rapidly losing his grip. He and Louis were now thoroughly reconciled, and Thomas clung to his son. The elder Stevensons were often in Bournemouth during the next two and a half years, Thomas visibly failing and sometimes being nursed by his invalid son. The younger Stevensons lived first in lodgings, then in a rented house – then, from the end of April 1885, in a house on the cliffs of Westbourne bought by Thomas for Fanny. They changed its name from 'Sea View' to 'Skerryvore', after the great lighthouse designed by Thomas's brother Alan and built with Thomas's help.

Louis's Savile Club friends descended on him at Bournemouth, wearing out the invalid, as Fanny thought, with their lively talk and deep potations. Fanny was sometimes distressed, too, at the way in which Louis's parents would stay for long stretches at a time and tire him emotionally. Henley came, and Bob Stevenson, and Bob's sister Katharine, whose unhappy marriage to a man called de Mattos had already involved Louis in troublesome mediation. Colvin alone of Louis's old friends was heedful of Fanny's hints and careful in his behaviour. But there was a new friend whom Louis made at Bournemouth who was accepted with equal enthusiasm by both the Stevensons and soon had a chair of his own at Skerryvore which they were anxious to see filled as often as possible. This was Henry James, whose essay, 'The Art of Fiction', that had appeared in *Longman's Magazine* in September 1884, had both delighted Louis by its insistence on the novelist's artistic responsibilities and provoked him to friendly disagreement with some of the particular points it made. The essay had also included a highly complimentary reference to *Treasure Island.*

Bournemouth in the late nineteenth century, seen from Westcliff.

In an engagingly amicable expression of his points of disagreement with James, entitled 'A Humble Remonstrance' and published in *Longman's* in 1884 (and later included in *Memories and Portraits*), Louis gave his own theory of fiction. 'Life is monstrous, infinite, illogical, abrupt, and poignant; a work of art, in comparison, is neat, finite, self-contained, rational, flowing, and emasculate. Life imposes by brute energy, like inarticulate thunder; art catches the ear, among the far louder noises of experience like an air artificially made by a discreet musician.' James had insisted that the novelist really does 'compete with life'. Louis replied: 'A proposition of geometry does not compete with life; and a proposition of geometry is a fair and luminous parallel for a work of art. Both are reasonable, both untrue to the crude fact; both inhere in nature, neither represents it. The novel which is a work of art exists, not by its resemblances to life, which are forced and material, as a shoe must still consist of leather, but by its immeasurable difference from life, which is designed and significant, and is both the method and the meaning of the work.' In opposition to James's refusal to distinguish character and action, seeing both as bound up in a single organic unity, Louis distinguished 'first, the novel of adventure, which appeals to certain almost sensual and quite illogical tendencies in man; second, the novel of character, which appeals to our intellectual appreciation of man's foibles and mingled and inconstant motives; and third, the dramatic novel which deals with the same stuff as the serious theatre, and appeals to our emotional nature and moral judgment'. (In his own best work, however, Louis mingled these different kinds and so proved James's point.) He concludes with stressing his points of agreement with James and gives advice to the aspiring novelist which is very Jamesian: 'Let him choose a motive, whether of character or passion; carefully construct his plot so that every incident is an illustration of the motive and every property employed shall bear to it a near relation of congruity or contrast; ... pitch the key of conversation, not with any thought of how men talk in parlours, but with a single eye to the degree of passion he may be called on to express; and allow neither himself in the narrative nor any character in the course of the dialogue, to utter one sentence that is not part and parcel of the business of the story or the discussion of the problem involved.'

James was delighted to discover someone who could argue about fiction in his own terms, and wrote to Louis on 5 December 1884: 'It's a luxury, in this immoral age, to encounter some one who *does* write – who is really acquainted with that lovely art.' Louis replied on the eighth, hoping for a continuation of the debate. 'People suppose,' he wrote, 'it is "the stuff" that interests them; they think, for instance, that the prodigious fine sentiments in Shakespeare impress by their own weight, not understanding that the unpolished diamond is but a stone. They think that striking situations, or good dialogue, are got by studying life; they will not rise to understand that they are prepared by deliberate artifice and set off by painful suppressions. Now, I want the whole thing well ventilated, for my own education and the public's, and I beg you to look as quick as you can, to follow me up with every circumstance of defeat where we differ, and (to prevent the flouting of the laity) to emphasise the points where we agree.' He looked up to James as

Henry James.

Now with an outlandish grace,
To the sparkling fire I face
In the blue room at Skerryvore;
And I wait until the door
Open, and the Prince of men,
Henry James, shall come again.

(Conclusion of poem written to James, 7 March 1886)

the Master. 'I seem to myself a very rude, left-handed countryman; not fit to be read, far less complimented, by a man so accomplished, so adroit, so craftsmanlike as you.' It is important to remember, in an age when James is regarded as the exemplar of the novelist as practitioner of a high art and Stevenson is all too often relegated to the shelves reserved for children's writers, that James regarded Stevenson as a fellow artist and that the first really sophisticated exchange of ideas in English about the art of fiction took place between these two.

James first came to Bournemouth in late April 1885 to spend some weeks there with his invalid sister Alice. He, of course, visited Louis, and immediately a literary friendship blossomed into a lifetime's deep mutual affection. When Louis left Britain for ever, James alone of his London friends understood and appreciated Louis's need to settle in the South Seas and, though he deeply regretted his absence, never reproached him with it or assumed, as Gosse for example assumed, that any writer in the English language who lived more than three miles from Charing Cross was doomed to decline in both skill and reputation. He understood that in Samoa Louis could not only keep alive but keep both physically and mentally active, and he kept writing to him with unflagging affection and admiration. Louis's friendship with Charles Baxter had begun in youth and combined a joint nostalgia for their student days with Louis's dependence on Charles as his business man and financial agent. Charles was also a fellow Scot, and Louis indulged his Scottishness in writing to him. James was the friend of his maturity and ministered to different needs. Neither friendship, once begun, ever waned. These two devoted friends of Louis lived in different worlds, and Louis's profound attachment to each says something about the complexity of his character and the variety of his emotional needs.

Louis's three years at Bournemouth brought no improvement in his health, but the usual frightening sequence of haemorrhages and long convalescences. He spent a great deal of his time in bed. 'Remember the pallid brute that lived in Skerryvore like a weevil in a biscuit,' he was to write later from Samoa. He finished *Prince Otto* and *A Child's Garden of Verses*, wrote the short stories 'Markheim' and 'The Body Snatcher' (the latter a 'crawler' of a pretty sensational kind, showing Louis's sense of evil in a way that was considered rather shocking), *Kidnapped* (first serialized in *Young Folks*, May to July 1886, and then published the same year in book form) and *Strange Case of Dr Jekyll and Mr Hyde*. He also wrote his *Memoir of Fleeming Jenkin*, who died in June 1885. And he worked on plays with Henley and planned a variety of other work.

Kidnapped is Stevenson's great topographical novel, the true vindication of his insistence on a sense of place in certain kinds of fiction. It is also in its way a historical novel and a psychological novel probing the differences between Lowland and Highland mentality and sensibility. From its beautifully simple opening, describing in the first person the young hero's departure from his father's house for the last time on a quiet June morning, through its cumulative series of adventures that get young David involved with the Highlander Alan Breck and so in the history of the Highlands just after the

An illustration from *Kidnapped*, as serialized in *Young Folks*.

defeat of the Jacobite Rebellion of 1745, the story moves with wonderful assurance and perfectly controlled changes of tone. The whole tragic atmosphere of the mid-eighteenth-century Highlands is expressed, but the tragedy never enters fully into the fabric of the novel, being subordinated to the line of adventure, the changing fortunes of the hero and his relation to his fellow fugitive. The moral problem is real and, as always in Stevenson, far from simple. The problem of an innocent man tried in his enemy's court and the linked problem of the duty of the innocently involved bystander in such a situation are searchingly presented, as is the combination of shiftiness and courage and charm in the character of Alan Breck, but none of this interferes with the rapid flow of the narrative. And the confident handling of the first-person narrative enables the author to show the temptations and weaknesses of his hero without our losing our admiration for him. There is something else important about *Kidnapped*: it provided an 'objective correlative' of one set of feelings about Scotland that had been germinating in Louis for a long time (just as his last, unfinished novel, *Weir of Hermiston*, going even further back in his own memories, embodied another and yet deeper set of feelings about Scotland). Significantly, he dedicated *Kidnapped* to Baxter. '. . . Sir, it's Scotch:' he wrote him, 'no strong, for the sake o' they pork-puddens, but jist a kitchen o't, to leeven the wersh, sapless, fushionless, stotty, stytering South-Scotch they think sae muckle o'. Its name is *Kidnaaapped; or Memoyers of the Adventyers of David Balfour in the Year Seventeen Hunner and Fifty Wan.* There's nae sculduddery aboot that, as ye can see for yourself.' (Charles was delighted and touched with Louis's proposal to dedicate the book to him. 'A book lives while we are dead,' he wrote to Louis, 'and it does seem something that the memory of a friendship which I think, my dear boy, has been singularly uncrossed by cloud should somewhere live embalmed in a kindly message from one to other.')

William Archer.

Strange Case of Dr Jekyll and Mr Hyde, published in January 1886, sold forty thousand copies in Britain during the first six months, and then innumerably more in America in both authorized and pirated editions. As Louis's cousin and first biographer, Graham Balfour, recorded, 'Its success was probably due rather to the moral instincts of the public than to any conscious perception of the merits of its art. It was read by those who never read fiction, it was quoted in pulpits, and made the subject of leading articles in religious newspapers.' It is of course a story about good and evil subsisting within the same person and shows Louis's lifelong fascination with the ambiguities of the individual moral character. The events are deployed with remarkable skill, the manipulation of the time-scheme and the changes in point of view building up to a discovery of the tragedy without the reader's yet fully understanding it, the understanding being given only in the doctor's autobiographical account that follows. The fact that Hyde, the doctor's stunted evil self, manifests his evil in acts of physical brutality rather than in, say, sexual license, although the moral defectiveness to which he owed his release relates to the kind of hedonistic adventurism that Stevenson himself practised in his bohemian days, is perhaps evidence of Stevenson's instinctive awareness of the relation between sensuality and sadism, but it is more likely to result from the impossibility in the 1880s of describing acts of violent sensuality with the frankness they require if they are to administer to the reader the kind of shock which the story demands. Nevertheless, Hyde's physical brutalities are symbolic in scope and stand for a whole world of evil. The story is powerful and indeed sensational, but at the same time it shows the deep kind of insight into the dualities and hypocrisies bred by Calvinism that Burns had shown in a different way in 'Holy Willie's Prayer' and James Hogg had shown in a not dissimilar way in his masterpiece, *Memoirs of a Justified Sinner*.

Among the writers Louis got to know during his Bournemouth period was William Archer, who reviewed *A Child's Garden* enthusiastically in March 1885, but subsequently wrote an article on his work in general dubbing him an 'athletico-aesthete' and warning him that if he had ever been really ill he would see the world differently. This amused rather than angered Louis, and provoked a correspondence in which Louis revealed his own view of himself. 'Why have I not written my *Timon*? Well, here is my worst quarrel with you. You take my young books as my last word. The tendency to try to say more has passed unperceived (my fault, that). And you make no allowance for the slowness with which a man finds and tries to learn his tools. I began with a neat brisk little style, and a sharp little knock of partial observation; I have tried to expand my means, but still I can only utter a part of what I wish to say, and am bound to feel; and much of it will die unspoken. But if I had the pen of Shakespeare, I have no *Timon* to give forth. I feel kindly to the powers that be; . . . To have suffered, nay, to suffer, sets a keen edge on what remains of the agreeable. This is a great truth, and has to be learned in the fire.' And in a postscript to another letter: 'To me, the medicine bottles on my chimney and the blood on my handkerchief are accidents; they do not colour my view of life, as you would know, I think, if you had experience of sickness; they do not exist in my prospect; I would as soon drag them under the eyes of my readers as I might mention a pimple I might chance to have (saving your presence) on my posteriors.'

Fanny's care for her husband not only involved her in disputes with those of his friends who had known him in his gay bachelor days: periodically she succeeded in falling out with Louis, too, when her worry about him manifested itself in gloom and nagging. 'My wife is peepy and dowie,' Louis wrote to James in January 1887: 'two Scotch expressions with which I will leave you to wrestle unaided, as a preparation for my poetical works. She is a woman (as you know) not without art: the art of extracting the gloom of the eclipse from sunshine; and she has recently laboured in this field not without success or (as we used to say) not without a blessing. It is strange: "we fell out my wife and I" the other night; she tackled me savagely for being a canary-bird; I replied (bleatingly) protesting that there was no use in turning life into King Lear; presently it was discovered that there were two dead combatants upon the field, each slain by an arrow of truth, and we tenderly carried off each other's corpses.' He ended with greetings 'from the Tragic Woman and the Flimsy Man'. Archer was thus not the only person who resented Louis's willed cheerfulness. But it is clearly what kept him going. Again and again in the letters we find humorous verses, lively Scottish vernacular humour (to Baxter), invented comic incidents and grave exaggerations of real events, often written between appalling bouts of haemorrhaging or even while seeping blood. 'Perpetually and exquisitely amusing as he was,' James wrote after his death in reviewing his *Letters to his Family and Friends*, 'his ambiguities and compatibilities yielded, for all the wear and tear of them, endless "fun" even to himself; and no one knew so well with what linked diversities he was saddled, or – to put it the other way – how many horses he had to drive at once.' This is highly perceptive. Stevenson's letters do not show the heroic invalid of sentimental legend but the reluctant pragmatist who accepted the universe not because it was the best of all possible worlds but because it was the only one he knew and therefore had to be made the best of. His letters, which James regarded as belonging 'with the very first' in this literary form, could, taken together, arguably be regarded as his finest work.

On 8 May 1887 Thomas Stevenson died. Louis had gone up to Edinburgh when he heard how critically ill his father was, but he arrived too late. He was not allowed to attend the funeral, as he had caught a cold, and was confined to the house until the end of the month, when he returned to Bournemouth. In August *Underwoods*, his second volume of verse, was published. Louis had written verse virtually all his life, and continued to do so, but he had no illusions about his poetic gifts. He was an accomplished versifier, and could be graceful and witty and amusing and nostalgic and pleasingly descriptive or complimentary or consolatory in verse. Apart from *A Child's Garden*, which as we have seen had special qualities, his greatest verse successes lay in capturing a mood deftly and economically, and he often did this best in Scots (Book II of *Underwoods* contains poems in Scots – 'Lallan' as he called it, 'Lallans' as we now call it). Louis's poems in Scots are of importance to the biographer, as they identify very precisely the sources and varieties of his Scottish feeling; they also show him working with some skill and discipline in a tradition that generally manifested itself in the nineteenth century as debased and sentimentalized Burns.

With Thomas Stevenson's death, Louis felt no further obligation to remain in Britain and felt free to go where his health required. The depressingly frequent crises of haemorrhaging and speechlessness which were liable to follow even the slightest cold indicated that even the relatively mild climate of Bournemouth was too much for him. His uncle Dr George Balfour recommended Colorado, and Louis's Bournemouth doctor concurred. So, having persuaded his mother to accompany them, Louis decided to go to America. He received £3,000 under his father's will (there were difficulties about Thomas's estate that manifested themselves even before his death, and Louis eventually got less than people believed he would inherit) and his writings were now making money. (It should be added that during Thomas's lifetime Louis had cost his father a total of about £10,000; he was very conscious of his having lived on his father's bounty.)

'We – my mother, my wife, my stepson, my maidservant, and myself, five souls – leave, if all is well, Aug. 20th, per Wilson line SS. *Ludgate Hill*,' wrote Louis to his old friend the American artist Will Low on 6 August. The maid was Valentine Roch, a French-Swiss girl whom they had first engaged at Hyères. The party spent a day in London after leaving Bournemouth, and there Louis's friends came to say good-bye. Henry James sent a case of champagne on board as a remedy for seasickness. The ship sailed from Tilbury on 21 August. It was, though neither Louis nor his friends knew it, his last farewell to Britain: he was never to return to Europe. The *Ludgate Hill* put in at Le Havre to take on a consignment of a few apes and numerous horses, and Louis went ashore to write a brief note to Henry James on the headed writing-paper of the 'Grand Hotel & Bains Frascati': 'It is a fine James, & a very fine Henry James, and a remarkably fine wine; and as for the boat, it is a dam bad boat, and we are all very rough mariners.'

It was taken as a good omen that when the New York pilot came aboard on 6 September his name proved to be Hyde. Better still, when they landed the next day they found that Louis's reputation was established, for a crowd of reporters awaited him, as well as Will Low. The Stevenson party went to stay with friends in Newport, but Louis caught a cold on the journey and spent most of the fortnight's stay in bed. He returned to New York to meet publishers and editors and arrange terms for books and articles. He was in demand, and was able to bargain. He agreed to write twelve articles a year for *Scribner's Magazine* for an annual £700. Having established his financial base, he thought of where to settle down. Colorado now seemed too far and uncertain; Saranac Lake in the Adirondack Mountains had just come into prominence as good for the tubercular, and accordingly this was decided on as the next Stevenson place of abode. Fanny and Lloyd went first, to find a house for the winter, and Louis and his mother followed, arriving on 3 October. 'I am at Saranac Lake in the Adirondacks, I suppose for the winter,' Louis wrote to Gosse on 8 October, 'it seems a first-rate place; we have a

Lloyd (centre), Fanny and Louis on the veranda of the house in which they stayed at Saranac Lake during the winter of 1887–88.

house in the eye of many winds, with a view of a piece of running water – Highland, all but the dear hue of peat – and of many hills – Highland also, but for the lack of heather.' Dr Trudeau, the tuberculosis expert of Saranac, examined Louis and found no active disease present, but evidence of previous and the chance of future attacks. Louis must have been reasonably well to have survived the bitterly cold winter in fairly primitive conditions, dressed, when he went out for his daily walk, in buffalo coat, astrakhan cap and Indian boots that Fanny had gone to Montreal to buy. In March 1888 he wrote to Colvin that, strangely enough, 'this harsh, grey, glum, doleful climate has done me good'. But he did find conditions hard. 'When the thermometer stays all day below 10°, it is really cold; and when the wind blows, O commend me to the result. Pleasure in life is all delete; there is no red spot left, fires do not radiate, you burn your hands all the time on what seem to be cold stones.' But he was able to work. Apart from his essays for *Scribner's*, he was engaged on *The Master of Ballantrae*, having got the inspiration from the impact of the Adirondack scene on 'a story conceived long before on the moors between Pitlochry and Strathairdle, conceived in Highland rain, in the blend of the smell of heather and bog-plants, and with a mind full of the Athole correspondence and the Memoirs of the Chevalier de Johnstone [relating to the Jacobite Rebellion of 1745]. So long ago, so far away it was, that I had first evoked the faces and the mutual tragic situation of the men of Durrisdeer.' He worked at it with enthusiasm that winter, but it was not completed when he left Saranac in April. It was finished later in Tahiti and Hawaii and published in 1889, after serialization in *Scribner's* from November 1888 to October 1889.

Standing statue of Louis by D. W. Stevenson, in the Glasgow Museum.

Bronze plaque by Augustus Saint Gaudens, showing Louis in bed in New York, 1887.

YOUTH NOW FLEES ON FEATHERED FOOT
FAINT AND FAINTER SOUNDS THE FLUTE
RARER SONGS OF GODS AND STILL
SOMEWHERE ON THE SUNNY HILL
OR ALONG THE WINDING STREAM
THROUGH THE WILLOWS FLITS A DREAM
FLITS BUT SHOWS A SMILING FACE
FLEES BUT WITH SO QUAINT A GRACE
NONE CAN CHOOSE TO STAY AT HOME
ALL MUST FOLLOW ALL MUST ROAM

AVGVSTVS · SAINT GAVDENS

Y · SHE
ND FREE
THE BLUE
ON FLEW
AND WET
S AND SET
E ROOF
ALOOF
DS AND KISS'T
THYST

LANE
IN VAIN
E CHASE
FACE
UMBLE ON
GONE

TY LED
DEAD
AY
OSE WAY

Louis knew that in *The Master of Ballantrae* he was on to something good. He wrote to Colvin on 24 December 1887 that he had 'fallen head over heels into a new tale' and added: 'It seems to me a most seizing tale: there are some fantastic elements; the most is a dead genuine human problem – human tragedy, I should say rather'. The following March he wrote to Henry James:

My novel is a tragedy; four parts out of six or seven are written, . . . Five parts of it are sound, human tragedy; that last one or two, I regret to say, not so soundly designed; I almost hesitate to write them; they are very picturesque, but they are fantastic; they shame, perhaps degrade, the beginning. I wish I knew; that was how the tale came to me however. . . . The older brother goes out in the '45, the younger stays; the younger, of course, gets title and estate and marries the bride designate of the elder – a family match, but he (the younger) had always loved her, and she had really loved the elder. Do you see the situation? . . . The elder brother is an INCUBUS: supposed to be killed at Culloden, he turns up again and bleeds the family of money; on that stopping he comes and lives with them, whence flows the real tragedy, the nocturnal duel of the brothers (very naturally, and indeed, I think, inevitably arising), and second supposed death of the elder. Husband and wife now really make up, and then the cloven hoof appears. For the third supposed death and manner of the third reappearance is steep; steep, sir. It is even very steep, and I fear it shames the honest stuff so far; but then it is highly pictorial, and it leads up to the death of the elder brother at the hands of the younger in a perfectly cold-blooded murder, of which I wish (and mean) the reader to approve. You see how daring is the design.

The manner of the elder brother's reappearance is indeed 'steep', and yet the fantastic element in it somehow moves on the same level of probability as the rest of the story – a triumph of achieved tone on Stevenson's part. The narrative is put into the mouth of a loyal and humble family retainer, a totally unheroic figure whose quietly tragic account and simple character contrast both with the seductive brilliance of the evil elder brother (the Master) and the patient worth of the morally admirable but less attractive younger. The attractiveness of evil if accompanied by style and *panache* and the hard lot of unspectacular virtue is a central theme in the novel. The linking of action to atmosphere and of both to landscape – the first and most brilliant part of the novel is set in south-west Scotland – is impressive. Stevenson is steadily learning how to bring together in an organic whole his interests in adventure, topography and moral ambiguities. Except for the controversial final part, which he kept referring to as 'that damned ending' and remained uneasy about, *The Master of Ballantrae* is a masterly work, the product of a full-fledged novelist realizing his powers. Henley called it 'grimy', and Louis countered that it was grim, not grimy. *The Master of Ballantrae*, he wrote to Colvin in January 1889, 'contains more human work than anything of mine but *Kidnapped*'. The modern reader is inclined to omit the qualification.

Some of the essays Louis wrote for *Scribner's* at Saranac show him developing his earlier attempts to work out a moral and religious creed based on a clear-eyed acceptance of the uncertainties and contradictions in the human condition. The most impressive of these is 'Pulvis et Umbra', first printed in *Scribner's Magazine* (April 1888) and in book form in *Across the Plains*

But while Joseph Finsbury was gaining for himself a
name among the more cultivated portion of the ignorant, his
domestic life was much interrupted by the death of his
youngest brother Jacob, who left him guardian to his two
sons Morris and John. At about the same time his family
was increased by the addition of a little girl who was left
in his charge on the death of John Henry Hazeltine Esq -- a
gentleman of small property and fewer friends. Having once
met Joseph at a lecture in the Royal Institution, was
so much impressed by his remarkable powers of mind and of
conversation that he appointed him in his will, sole guardian to his little daughter.

Although Joseph at first refused to take the little
girl, his natural pity for one so small and friendless over-
ruled his premature refusal; he reluctantly advertised for a
nurse, and invested in a second hand perambulator. On the
other hand he was delighted to take charge of the two father-
less little boys, and their fortune of thirty thousand pounds;
the leather business received a great spurt by the in-
vestment therein of a considerable part of his wards' money.
A young but capable Scot was chosen as manager to the en-
terprise, and the cares of business never again afflicted
Joseph Finsbury.Leaving his charges in the care of the
capable Scot (who was married) he began his extensive
travels on the continent, and in Asia Minor.

Lloyd Osbourne and (*left*) his typescript of *The Wrong Box*, with handwritten corrections by Louis.

(1892). He has few illusions. He contemplates the earth, 'loaded with pre-
datory life, and more drenched with blood, both animal and vegetable, than
ever mutinied ship', as it 'scuds through space with unimaginable speed, and
turns alternate cheeks to the reverberation of a blazing world, ninety million
miles away'. He sees man, 'of all earth's meteors, . . . the most strange and
consoling: that this enobled lemur, this hair-crowned bubble of the dust, this
inheritor of a few years and sorrows, should yet deny himself his rare delights,
and add to his frequent pains, and live for an ideal, however misconceived'.
He sets this bundle of contradictions living 'in his isle of terror and under the
imminent hand of death' in the green world of nature and the strangely
diverse world of other animals and sees no comfort except what can be wrung
by man's determination not to despair of unrewarded effort or utter the
language of complaint. The most that can be expected is, in the words of
'A Christmas Sermon', another essay written at this time and also printed
first in *Scribner's* and then in *Across the Plains*, what he called 'faithful failure'.
'To be honest, to be kind – to earn a little and to spend a little less, to make
upon the whole a family happier for his presence, to renounce when that
shall be necessary and not be embittered, to keep a few friends but these
without capitulation – above all, on the same grim condition, to keep friends
with himself – here is a task for all that a man has of fortitude and delicacy.'
This may seem at first sight to represent a creed both simple-minded and
conventional, but if we look at it properly in its context we can see that it
represents the wry Stoicism that underlay all Stevenson's views of man.

Lloyd also had ambitions as a writer and it was at Saranac that he began
that complexly farcical story entitled *The Wrong Box* and published in
1889. Louis then took over and rewrote Lloyd's draft. It was the first of

W. E. Henley.

Louis's collaborations with his stepson, the most sustained product of which was to be *The Wrecker*, an adventure story almost picaresque in the looseness of its construction but containing, in Louis's part, some interesting and revealing autobiographical elements. *The Wrecker*, serialized in *Scribner's* in 1891–92 and published in book form in the latter year, was one of a series of 'South Sea Yarns' which Louis and Lloyd planned to write together: it was better received than *The Wrong Box*, which appealed to Louis's sense of comic extravaganza, but which to most readers has always seemed laboured and dull. It is odd that a writer of Louis's individuality accepted the idea of collaboration so readily – with his wife as well as with his stepson. Lloyd later described his collaboration with Louis as 'a mistake for me, nearly as much as for him; but I don't believe Louis ever enjoyed any work more. He liked the comradeship – my work coming in just as his energy flagged, or *vice versa*; and he liked my applause when he – as he always did – pulled us magnificently out of sloughs.'

Life at Saranac was quiet, and Louis's health benefited. When spring came he felt able to consider putting into practice a plan that had been forming in his mind for many months. This was to charter a yacht and undertake a long sea voyage. His mother, who had proved a good sailor on the transatlantic crossing, liked the idea. Fanny was happy about it. Lloyd was excited. And the maid, Valentine Roch, was willing. Fanny visited her native Indiana in March and then proceeded to San Francisco with instructions to see about hiring a yacht there. Louis went to New York, where he met Mark Twain, and then, with his mother and Lloyd, spent a month in Manasquan, New Jersey. He was there when a telegram arrived from Fanny saying that the yacht *Casco* could be hired, with Captain Otis in command, for a trip among the islands of the South Seas. On 28 May 1888 Louis wrote 'a valedictory' to Henry James. 'On June 15th the schooner yacht *Casco* will (jealous providence permitting) steam through the Golden Gates for Honolulu, Tahiti, the Galapagos, Guayaquil, and – I hope *not* the bottom of the Pacific. It will contain your obedient 'umble servant and party. It seems too good to be true, and is a very good way of getting through the green-sickness of maturity which, with all its accompanying ills, is now declaring itself in my mind and life.' Early in June Louis and his party joined Fanny in California. A seven months' voyage was planned. The hire of the yacht cost Louis £2,000, which he took out of the £3,000 he had got from his father's estate. The American editor and publisher S. S. McClure (who had in 1884 established the first syndicate to provide material for newspapers throughout the country) offered handsome payment for a series of letters describing his experiences during the voyage.

So began Louis's involvement with the South Seas, which was to last for the short remainder of his life and leave a permanent mark on his literary character and reputation. 'I am never well but at sea,' he once wrote, and sea voyaging was certainly good for both his morale and his physique. And Polynesia proved to have a climate in which he could live without the constant threat of upper respiratory infection, with its consequence in haemorrhaging. He had – or so it appeared – found a way of keeping alive, and he stuck to it. But he was leaving behind more than the civilization of Europe and America when the *Casco,* after several delays, finally sailed from San Francisco on 28 June 1888. He was also trying to exorcize the memory of a bitter quarrel with Henley which had blown up suddenly the preceding March.

It had begun with a letter from Henley to Louis (marked 'Private and Confidential') on 9 March. The letter opened with his usual affectionate address, 'Dear Boy'. Henley reproached Louis, but in a friendly enough way, for his view of life; he himself considered life to be 'uncommonly like rot'. He complained of feeling 'out of key'. And he expressed dissatisfaction with his own recent work. Then, in one short paragraph, he referred to a story that Fanny had had published in the March issue of *Scribner's,* which he said he had read 'with considerable amazement'. Surely it was Katharine's story (Katharine de Mattos, Bob Stevenson's sister), even though in some degree rewritten, 'and why there wasn't a double signature is what I've not been able to understand'. Then, as though accusing Louis's wife of outright plagiarism was not an intolerable insult, especially to a man as sensitive on such things as Louis, Henley went rambling on to other matters. But he must have known what he was doing, for his last sentence was: 'Forgive this babble, and take care of yourself, and *burn this letter.*'

Katharine de Mattos: anonymous watercolour.

Louis did not burn the letter. He replied in cold anger, perfectly controlled in outwardly polite language, reminding Henley that Katharine had consented to Fanny's using her idea and had not wanted either to collaborate or to have her name on Fanny's version. He then asked Henley not only to withdraw his accusation against Fanny but, if he had spoken of the matter to others, to provide 'a proper explanation of what you shall have said or implied to any person so addressed'. He urged Henley to apply to Katharine for the facts, which would enable him to see how wrong he was. Meanwhile: 'You will pardon me if I can find no form of signature; I pray God such a blank will not be of long endurance.' And he signed himself simply 'Robert Louis Stevenson'. Louis then wrote to Charles Baxter telling him what had happened and saying, 'I fear I have come to an end with Henley'. The letter makes clear that Henley's accusation against Fanny was merely the last straw in a series of provocative actions against him by Henley. He had kept quiet and forgiven up till now, 'for I understand all his nature, and much of it I love'. It is a long letter, 'a very desolate cry', as Louis called it in a postscript. Henley remained silent, communicating with Louis on a business matter through a third party, and Louis wrote him briefly at the end of March saying that he would not raise the other matter again and if Henley did not want to write, 'it is perhaps better for you to let it alone'. But this time he signed himself 'still and always, if I never saw your face again – Yours affectionately, Robert Louis Stevenson'. But on 5 April he wrote to Charles saying that he had heard from Katharine and that her letter showed the case to be 'worse than ever'. He now saw Katharine as behind Henley, and despaired. Yet he longs for a reconciliation with his old friend. Charles wrote at length to Louis asking him to bear with Henley. 'Remember *everything,* Louis my friend, and forget, forget only to think of parting with one who would, I verily believe, give his life in your service.' But Henley did not write his retraction, and on 10 April Louis wrote to Charles of his continued distress. 'How I wish I had died at Hyères, where all was well with me!' Finally, on 11 April, Henley wrote. He pointed out that the business letter sent through a third party was written 'before there had dawned upon me any suspicion that my remarks [on Fanny's story] could possibly go near to turning our lives into separate tragedies'. He concludes: 'Forgive me, and have faith in me yet. I am not ungrateful nor disloyal.' But he does not apologize or retract. Henley wrote again on 7 May, admitting that Louis's last letter, which he found 'heart-breaking', had convicted him '(I now see) of a piece of real unkindness, unworthy of myself and our old true friendship'. But he provided no withdrawal of his charge against Fanny. '. . . Even if he still thinks as he did, I think a kind spirit would have even lied,' Louis concluded his note written at the top of Henley's letter.

Henley did not get on with Fanny, who disliked and suspected him, and whom he in turn disliked. He never forgave her for having changed the Louis that he knew. He also resented Louis's staying in America. It is clear that he had been offending Louis for some time before this crisis, but Louis, who really did love the man though he was becoming increasingly irritated with him, bore with him. But an attack on his wife's honour was not to be borne, least of all by someone of Louis's sensitivity both about honour and about his wife's reputation among his old male friends. This was something which Henley never fully realized. The breach was never completely healed, though Louis said many generous things about Henley afterwards. He wrote later that he expected that after both were dead some young magazine writer would 'expose the horrid R.L.S. and at last do justice to the misused W.E.H. For he is of that big, round, human, faulty stamp of man that makes lovers after death. I bet he has drunk more, and smoked more, and talked more sense, and quarrelled with more friends, than any of God's creatures.' What Louis did not anticipate was that it would be Henley himself who would, after Louis's death, 'expose the horrid R.L.S'. Henley reviewed the official life of Stevenson, written by Graham Balfour and published in 1901, in *The Pall Mall Gazette*. The review was an appalling outburst of spleen, not only a protest that Balfour's picture, 'this Seraph in Chocolate, this barley-sugar effigy of a real man', was not 'my old, riotous, intrepid, scornful Stevenson at all', but a bitter accusation against Louis of vanity, affectation, unscrupulousness and condescension. Henley had interpreted a somewhat garbled extract from a letter of Louis's that Balfour printed in his *Life* as an insult by Louis to him. This, working on his old hostility to Fanny, his jealousy of Louis's success and popularity and his feeling that America and marriage and the South Seas had corrupted Louis, produced an explosive mixture that resulted in one of the most extraordinary posthumous attacks on a writer by his friend known in our literature.

Fanny wrote to Baxter from San Francisco in fury not only against Henley but against all Louis's friends in Britain and against 'perfidious Albion': she was in a state of hysterical bitterness. A somewhat calmer letter followed, but she still said, 'The injury can never be condoned nor do I ever wish to see

The schooner *Casco*.

England again.' On 28 May Louis wrote to Baxter, 'O, I go on my journey with a bitter heart. It will be best for all, I daresay, if the *Casco* goes down with me. For there's devilish little left to live for.' But later, after saying how he is haunted by Henley's letter, he says, 'Well, I mean to beat the wind. I *will* have a good time on the *Casco*. It means a hard heart; well, harden it, O Lord! and let's be done.'

The *Casco* proved good therapy. In spite of Captain Otis's doubts about having such a mixed group of landlubbers on board, and in spite of Fanny's seasickness, everyone soon settled down and as the ship sailed south Louis's spirits rose. He recaptured his state of mind in chapter twelve of *The Wrecker*: 'Day after day, the air had the same indescribable liveliness and sweetness, soft and nimble, and cool as the cheek of health. Day after day, the sun flamed; night after night the moon beaconed, or the stars paraded their lustrous regiment. I was aware of a spiritual change, or perhaps, rather a molecular reconstitution. My bones were sweeter to me. I had come to my own climate, and looked back with pity on those damp and wintry zones, miscalled the temperate.' Yet at the same time as Louis was renewing himself physically and mentally as he sailed further and further away from the temperate zone, his imagination was haunted by visions and memories of his Scottish past. Indeed, it is the tension between memory and new experience, between nostalgia and present commitment, that provides the clue to the way the later Stevenson's imagination often worked. On 6 September he wrote to Baxter from 'Yacht Casco, at sea, near the Paumotus' about a sudden vision he had had of Drummond Place (in the New Town of Edinburgh) and Rutherford's, the pub he had frequented as a student. In the same letter he says, 'I shall have a fine book of travels, I feel sure.' On 10 November he writes Baxter from Tautira enclosing 'my attempt at words to "Wandering Willie"', beginning

> *Home no more home to me, whither shall I wander?*
>   *Hunger my driver, I go where I must.*
> *Cold blows the winter wind over hill and heather;*
>   *Thick drives the rain, and my roof is in the dust.*
> *Loved of wise men was the shade of my roof-tree,*
>   *The true word of welcome was spoken in the door.*
> *Dear days of old, with the faces in the firelight,*
>   *Kind folks of old, you come again no more.*

On 28 July the *Casco* dropped anchor in Anaho Bay, the harbour of the island of Nukahiva in the Marquesas. This was Louis's first landfall in the islands of the South Seas, and it made an indelible impression on him. They approached in early dawn, 'the customary thrill of landfall heightened by the strangeness of the shores that we were then approaching. Slowly they took shape in the attenuating darkness. Uahuna, piling up to a truncated summit, appeared the first upon the starboard bow; almost abeam arose our destination, Nukahiva, whelmed in cloud; and betwixt, and to the southward, the first rays of the sun displayed the needles of Uapu. These pricked about the line of the horizon, like the pinnacles of some ornate and monstrous church; they stood there, in the sparkling brightness of the morning, the fit signboard of a world of wonders'. They lay for three weeks in Anaho Bay, and Louis made his first acquaintance with the life of the South Sea islanders. The natives of the Marquesas, cannibals until recently, had had their vigorous and often barbaric customs tamed by an inefficient French colonial administration; they were now a rapidly dwindling and culturally confused population. Louis and his party impressed them enormously, for here was a rich white man sailing purely for pleasure with his own entourage. They gave him the honorific title of 'Ona' (that is, owner). Louis explored and fraternized; exchanged courtesies with local chiefs; spoke French with the administrators and the better-educated natives; and accumulated new impressions and new knowledge. 'I chose these isles as having the most beastly population, and they are far better and far more civilized than we,' he wrote to Colvin. 'I know one old chief Ko-o-amua, a great cannibal in his day, who ate his enemies even as he walked home from killing 'em, and he is a perfect gentleman and exceedingly amiable and simple-minded: no fool, though.'

On 21 September he reported progress to Colvin:

Get out your big atlas, and imagine a straight line from San Francisco to Anaho, the N.E. corner of Nukahiva, one of the Marquesas Islands; imagine three weeks there: imagine a day's sail on August 12th round the eastern end of the island to Tai-o-hae, the capital; imagine us there till August 22nd: imagine us skirt the east side of Ua-pu – perhaps Rona-Poa on your atlas – and through the Bondelais straits to Taaka-uku in Hiva-Oa, where we arrive on the 23rd; imagine us there until September 4th, when we sailed for Fakarava, which we reached on the 9th, after a very difficult and dangerous passage among these isles. Tuesday, we shall leave for Taiti, where I shall knock off and do some necessary work ashore. It looks pretty bald in the atlas; not in fact; nor I trust in the 130 odd pages of diary which I have just been looking up for these dates: the interest, indeed, has been *incredible*: I did not dream there were such places or such races. My health has stood me splendidly; I am in the water for hours wading over the knees for shells; I have been five hours on horseback: I have been up pretty near all night waiting to see where the *Casco* would go ashore, and with my diary all ready – simply the most entertaining night of my life.

He still caught colds, however, sometimes severe ones, and on Fakarava in the Paumotus developed a particularly threatening one, which led to the party cutting short their stay there and sailing on to Papeete, the principal town of Tahiti. They spent some time in a small house at Papeete, where Louis's condition fluctuated, then moved on to Taravo on the south side of the island and thence, in a wagon owned by a local Chinese, to the village of Tautira, sixteen miles away. There they were graciously entertained by the important female chief 'Princess' Moë and, as a result of her influence, were lent a European-style house by the sub-chief Teriitera (otherwise known as Ori à Ori). Louis and Fanny ceremonially exchanged names respectively with Teriitera and Moë, thus confirming their acceptance as socially important visitors. The discovery of dry rot in the masts of the *Casco* meant that they had to stay at Tautira until the end of December while Captain Otis got the necessary repairs done at Papeete. Louis's health improved, he indulged his habitual curiosity about native life and customs and established ever more cordial relations with his host, and he started work again on *The Master of*

Lloyd, Fanny, Louis, King
Kalakaua and Mrs Thomas
Stevenson in the cabin of the *Casco*.

Ballantrae, nearly finishing it. On Christmas Day 1888 the Stevensons re-
embarked on the repaired *Casco* and set sail for Honolulu. It was a wearisome
voyage, with alternating calms and contrary winds, and they did not arrive
at Honolulu until the end of January. There Belle and Joe Strong (who had
married in 1879) were waiting for them, as well as some much-needed money.
Louis dismissed the *Casco*, and settled down to six months of living on shore.

'My wife is no great shakes: she is the one who has suffered most. My mother
has had a Huge Old Time. Lloyd is first chop. I so well that I do not know
myself. . . .' So Louis wrote to Baxter from Honolulu on 8 February. The
only loss to the little group now was Valentine Roch, who returned to
California where she married. She appears not to have got on with Fanny:
Louis recorded her departure 'to mutual glee'. The group settled themselves
at Waikiki in somewhat makeshift housing. The Strongs, who had now been
living for some time in Honolulu, with their small son Austin, had formed
close connections with King Kalakaua and the assorted royal ménage that
played an important part in the social and political life of Hawaii. Louis got
on extremely well with the King and his friends, and from now on became
increasingly involved in island problems and island politics. He generously
espoused his new friends' views, which involved him in Samoan politics
too, for Kalakaua had sent an 'embassy' to Samoa, accompanied by an
antiquated gunboat manned by young criminals from the royal reform school,
to further his aim of an island federation led by Hawaii. Louis went so far as to
write a white-hot letter to *The Times* presenting the rebuff of this pathetic
mission as an affront to Hawaian dignity and giving the romanticized and
highly biased royal view of the situation in Samoa. But later he acquired a
fuller understanding of the realities of South Seas politics and the cultural
tragedy of Polynesia, caught between its own dying past and the indolently
greedy present of the Western powers. This fuller understanding was eventually manifested in *A Footnote to History*, published in 1892, which a modern
student of Polynesian history and society has called a 'classic in South Seas
history'.

In May Louis finally completed *The Master of Ballantrae*. In June he visited the leper settlement on the island of Molokai and spent seven days living among the lepers. It was an extraordinary experience, undertaken out of a compulsion to face what he called 'the horror of the horrible', only to find 'a horror of moral beauty' everywhere. He wrote to Fanny about his arrival among the 'hundreds of (God save us!) pantomime masks in poor human flesh':

Every hand was offered: I had gloves, but I had made up my mind on the boat's voyage *not* to give my hand, that seemed less offensive than the gloves. So the sisters and I went among that crew, and presently I got aside (for I felt I had no business there) and set off on foot across the promontory. . . . All horror was quite gone from me: to see these dread creatures smile and look happy was beautiful. On my way through Kalaupapa I was exchanging cheerful *alohas* with the patients coming galloping over on their horses; I was stopping to gossip at house-doors; I was happy, only ashamed of myself that I was here for no good. . . . Beyond Kalaupapa the houses became rare; dry stone dykes, grassy, stony land, one sick pandanus; a dreary country; from overhead in the little clinging wood shogs of the pali chirruping of birds fell; the low sun was right in my face; the trade wind blew pure and cool and delicious; I felt as right as ninepence, and stopped and chatted with the patients whom I still met on their horses, with not the least disgust.

To Colvin he wrote that 'the sight of so much courage, cheerfulness, and devotion strung me too high to mind the infinite pity and horror of the sights. . . . I have seen sights that cannot be told, and heard stories that cannot be repeated: yet I never admired my poor race so much, nor (strange as it may seem) loved life more than in the settlement'. Father Damien, the Catholic priest who had ministered devotedly on Molokai up to his death that April,

The church at the old leper settlement on the island of Molokai.

was much criticized by outsiders for his alleged immorality. Louis became interested in him. 'Of old Damien,' he wrote to Colvin, 'whose weakness and worse perhaps I heard fully, I think only the more. It was a European peasant: dirty, bigotted, untruthful, unwise, tricky, but superb with generosity, residual candour and fundamental good-humour.' Eight months later, in Sydney, he read in a church journal a denunciation of Damien by one Rev. Dr C. M. Hyde of Honolulu in the form of an answer to an inquiry about Damien by an Australian minister. This provoked Louis to white-hot fury and he produced his famous *Father Damien: An Open Letter to the Reverend Dr Hyde of Honolulu* (which first appeared in the *Australian Star*, Sydney, 24 May 1890), both a defence of Damien and a furious attack on Dr Hyde for his hypocritical sanctimoniousness and total lack of Christian charity and understanding. There had fused in Louis's mind the deep emotional experience of his days among the lepers and memories of earlier struggles to formulate his view of the true nature of Christian ethics against the 'unco' guid' bourgeois church-goers of Edinburgh. He thought he would be sued for libel, as he wrote to Baxter, and probably ruined. But this did not deter him from arranging for publication of the pamphlet in England.

In May Louis's mother left for Scotland. Having been unsuccessful in an attempt to get permission for his party to sail among the islands on the missionary ship *Morning Star*, Louis was able to get them passage on the new trading schooner *Equator*, which could accommodate the passengers and their plans while carrying on its normal trading in copra among the islands. Joe Strong joined the party, ostensibly to paint lantern slides that were to accompany a series of proposed money-making lectures about their journeyings to be given by Lloyd. Belle and little Austin were sent to Sydney to await the eventual arrival there of the rest of the group. Ah Fu, the Chinese cook shipped by the *Casco* in the Marquesas, who had remained with the Stevensons, was another member of the party who sailed for the Gilbert Islands in the *Equator* in June 1889.

Louis kept trying to explain to his friends why he was unable to come home. 'I feel as if I were untrue to friendship,' he wrote to Colvin in April; '. . . but I think you will pardon me if you consider how much this tropical weather mends my health. Remember me as I was at home, and think of me sea-bathing and walking about, jolly as a sandboy: you will own the temptation is strong; and as the scheme, bar fatal accidents, is bound to pay into the bargain, sooner or later, it seems it would be madness to come home now.' To Henry James, explaining in March that he was not coming home for another year, he owned he was 'untrue to friendship and (what is less, but still considerable) to civilization' and added: 'But look here, and judge me tenderly. I have had more fun and pleasure of my life these past months than ever before, and more health than any time in ten long years.' James alone understood. 'It's the best thing that can happen to one', he replied, 'to see it written in your very hand that you have been so uplifted in health and cheer, and if another year will screw you up so tight that you won't 'come undone' again, I will try and hold on through the barren months.' At the same time, he missed Louis 'shockingly'.

Samoan girl: watercolour by Joe Strong, 1891.

84

(*Left, above*) Pencil sketch, *The Cutter's Deck*, by Louis. (*Left, below*) Louis standing on the bowsprit of the trading schooner *Equator*. (*Opposite, above*) Apia at the end of the nineteenth century. (*Opposite, below*) King Tembinok' and his entourage leaving the trading-ship *Janet Nicoll* at the island of Apemama.

When they reached Apemama in the Gilbert Islands the Stevensons were determined to stay there for a time (while the *Equator* made her rounds to other islands, to return later and pick them up). This was not easy. Apemama was ruled by the formidable tyrant Tembinok', and it was only by some adroit manœuvring and clever one-upmanship in matters of local courtesy that they obtained Tembinok's permission to stay. All this, and his other remarkable experiences on these voyages, Louis wrote up with great verve (in spite of being pushed by both Fanny and Colvin to be less objective and more purely personal) in *In the South Seas*, first printed as a series of letters in the New York *Sun* in 1891 and then published in book form in 1896.

The natives of the Gilbert and Marshall Islands are Micronesians, differing in race and language from the Polynesians among whom Louis's previous experience of South Sea islanders lay and among whom it was to lie in the future. Tembinok' himself was an extraordinary man, a strong and complex character of many talents who had admitted missionaries to his island solely to learn English (of a sort) from them, and had then dismissed them. He arranged suitable accommodation for the Stevenson party and in the two months they spent there established a really affectionate relationship with Louis. Louis's own account of his departure is memorable:

As the time approached for our departure Tembinok' became greatly changed; a softer, more melancholy, and, in particular, a more confidential man appeared in his stead. To my wife he contrived laboriously to explain that though he knew he must lose his father in the course of nature, he had not minded nor realized it till the moment came; and that now he was to lose us, he repeated the experience. We showed fireworks one evening on the terrace. It was a heavy business; the sense of separation was in all our minds, and the talk languished. . . . Presently after we said good-night and withdrew; but Tembinok' detained Mr Osbourne, patting the mat by his side and saying: 'Sit down. I feel bad, I like talk.' 'You like some beer?' said he; and one of the wives produced a bottle. The king did not partake, but sat sighing and smoking a meerschaum pipe. 'I very sorry you go,' he said at last. 'Miss Stlevens he good man, woman he good man, boy he good man; all good man. Woman he smart all the same man. My woman,' glancing towards his wives, 'he good woman, no very smart. I think Miss Stlevens he big chiep all the same cap'n man-o'wa'. I think Miss Stlevens he rich man all the same me. All go schoona. I very sorry. My patha he go, my uncle he go, my cutcheons he go, Miss Stlevens he go: all go. You no see king cry before. King all the same man: feel bad, he cry. I very sorry.'

On 7 December 1889 the *Equator* reached Apia, capital and port of Upolu in the South Pacific group of islands known collectively as Samoa. There, with the help of an influential American trader called Harry J. Moors, they found a cottage to rent while they looked about them and arranged passage to Sydney. Shortly afterwards Moors had succeeded in selling the Stevensons the idea of buying and planting land on the slopes behind Apia. Moors was not a wholly disinterested party: he was to get a commission for arranging the clearing and building and importing necessaries and he had his own fish to fry which would be helped by Louis's presence as a planter on the island. Louis liked the idea of settling in a climate that was obviously good for his health – it was too humid at sea level but up on the slopes it was very agreeable

– and at the same time near a port that had good steamer connections with Australia, New Zealand and America. Fanny, who had always fancied herself as a pioneer, liked the idea of growing things in the tropics. So they were not put out by general doubts about the practicability of the various cash crops (cocoa, pineapple, vanilla) suggested, by the dubious labour situation, and by the even more dubious political situation, with which inevitably Louis soon got himself involved. By the time the Stevensons were embarked on the S.S. *Lübeck* for Sydney, at the beginning of February 1890, Louis was a landowner. He wrote to Baxter from the ship that he had 'bought 314½ acres of beautiful land in the bush behind Apia; when we get the house built, the garden laid, and cattle in the place, it will be something to fall back on for shelter and food; and if the island could stumble into political quiet, it is conceivable it might even bring a little income'. He paid ten dollars an acre, at seven dollars to the pound, and thus the land cost him about £400, though buildings, roads and other developments were eventually to cost him some £2,000 more. 'We range from 600 to 1500 feet, have 5 streams, waterfalls, precipices, profound ravines, rich tablelands, 50 head of cattle on the ground (if anyone could catch them [no-one ever did: they were probably non-existent]), a great view of forest, sea, mountains, the warships in the haven: really a noble place.' Actually, it had four streams, not five; but Louis liked the name Vailima, which (as Fanny explained to Baxter in an addition to Louis's letter) means 'the place of the five rivers', so they called it Vailima and pretended that it had five streams.

Louis intended to sail home and settle his affairs in Britain after a few months in Australia. But instead of receiving the eagerly awaited news of his return, Baxter received a telegram from Sydney dated 10 April: 'Return Islands four months Home September.' Louis had fallen seriously ill in Sydney, with fever, pleurisy and severe haemorrhaging, and it looked as though the only way to save his life was to get him back to sea among the islands. With considerable difficulty Fanny persuaded the owners of the small trading steamer *Janet Nicoll* to take on board the apparently dying man and his wife and stepson. They left on 10 April, chugging round the islands, calling at Suwarrow, visiting the new Stevenson property at Apia, and then on to the Gilbert and Marshall Islands again where Louis visited his friend Tembinok'. Louis rarely had much time on shore, for the *Janet Nicoll* was not a pleasure-boat but a trading-ship that could only spend a few hours at each place where she called. But it was the sea voyage that Louis needed. He wrote to Baxter on 20 May ('at sea, off Upolu') that the voyage had had 'the old effect', and whereas he had gone aboard straight from bed, a very sick man, 'a fortnight after I was ashore and cutting about on Savage Island, and having my pockets – (*proh pudor*) and my trouser pockets – picked of tobacco by the *houris* of that ilk, and sitting prating with missionaries, and clambering down cliffs to get photographs like a man of iron'.

On the return journey to Australia the *Janet Nicoll* put in at New Caledonia, where Louis exercised his French again and dined with the Governor in a comically improvised dress-suit. When he returned to Sydney in August he at once fell seriously ill again. So even the postponed September date for the

The last portrait photograph of
Louis.

Baptismal font made from
a coconut: a souvenir
collected by Louis.

visit home was now impossible. Louis wrote to Henry James from Sydney:
'I must tell you plainly – I can't tell Colvin – I do not think I shall come to
England more than once, and then it'll be to die. Health I enjoy in the tropics;
even here, which they call sub- or semi-tropics, I came only to catch cold. . . .
The thermometer was nearly down to 50° the other day – no temperature for
me, Mr James: how should I do in England? I fear not at all. I am sorry about
seven or eight people in England, and one or two in the States. And outside
of that, I simply prefer Samoa.' They were back in Samoa in October, and
Louis was settled there for life. It was Lloyd who went to England to arrange
Louis's affairs and to bring the furniture from Skerryvore to the still unbuilt
house on the mountainside. In January 1891 Louis sailed to Sydney – where
he fell 'sharply sick' – to meet his mother and bring her back to Samoa. But

the house was not ready when she arrived, and she went off to spend two months with relatives in New Zealand. But by May she was back in Samoa, installed in the Stevenson house, together with Belle Strong (now separated from her husband) and her son Austin. With Fanny and Lloyd and the Samoan servants and other retainers they progressively gathered round them, this made a large household, over which Louis henceforth presided with something of the air and the satisfaction of an old feudal landowner. As *Suenga* (Chief) of Vailima he had now achieved, though in a different culture, the same position that Sir Walter Scott achieved as Laird of Abbotsford. It was, as with Scott, in a sense an acting out of an ancestral role, and, again as with Scott, it was bound up with a deep surge of imaginative feeling about the past of his own country. But in Stevenson's case it was an exile's feeling.

Louis, with his family and household, outside Vailima, 31 July 1892.

The interior of Vailima.

The planning and building and progressive expansion of the house provided great excitement to the whole Stevenson household. Louis's cousin Graham Balfour came for a visit of several months in 1892, and he later gave a description of the house:

After December, 1892, the downstairs accommodation consisted of three rooms, a bath, a storeroom and cellars below, with five bedrooms and the library upstairs. On the groundfloor, a verandah, twelve feet deep, ran in front of the whole house and along one side of it. . . . Stevenson then had half of the open space boarded in, and used it as his own bedroom and study, the remainder of the verandah being sheltered, when necessary, by Chinese blinds. The new room was thus a sort of martin's nest, plastered as it were upon the outside of the house; . . . A small bedstead, a couple of bookcases, a plain deal kitchen table and two chairs were all its furniture, and two or three favourite Piranesi etchings and some illustrations of Stevenson's own works hung upon the walls. At one side was a locked rack containing halfadozen Colt's rifles for the service of the family in case they should ever be required. One door opened into the library, the other into the verandah; one window, having from its elevation the best view the house afforded, looked across the lawns and pasture, over the treetops, out to the sapphire sea, while the other was faced by the abrupt slope of Vaea [the mountain behind Vailima]. The library was lined with books, the covers of which had all been varnished to protect them from the climate. The most important divisions were the shelves allotted to the history of Scotland, to French books either modern or relating to the fifteenth century, to military history, and to books relating to the Pacific.

It was a silent house, for 'the sound of wheels or the din of machinery was hardly known in the island' and everyone went barefoot; but the distant beat of the surf was audible. Its chief feature was the large hall, about sixty feet by forty, occupying the whole of the ground floor, with walls and ceiling panelled with varnished redwood from California. This wooden house with its red roof of corrugated iron was in Polynesian eyes a palace, and the elegant furniture, silverware, glassware, portraits and mirrors from Skerryvore and

92

Heriot Row gave an air of old-world elegance to the pioneering building. Here the Stevensons entertained their guests to dinners and even public balls. These guests included different strata of the local population: there were half-Samoan products of mixed marriages and important white officials like the United States Consul, the United States and the British Land Commissioners (the latter was the brother of the novelist Rider Haggard), the German Consul, various missionaries, and of course friendly or admiring or simply curious visitors from outside. Louis also enjoyed entertaining officers and ratings from the British men-of-war stationed in Apia harbour. On social occasions Louis dressed elegantly in starched white mess jacket and pleated white silk shirt (from Sydney), while Fanny abandoned her usual loose sack-like garment for elegant gowns of silk or velvet. The Samoan servants served the guests with flowers in their hair and on very special occasions wore striped blazers and *lavalavas* (skirt made from a single length of cloth, originally introduced by the missionaries for reasons of modesty, often wrapped around the body from bosom to knee by Samoan women) in the Royal Stewart tartan, which Louis thought blended effectively with the colour of their skin.

Wash drawing of Vailima by Belle Strong, 22 June 1891.

93

Louis also entertained Samoan chiefs and retainers with the ceremonial courtesy that tradition required. He enjoyed these occasions, and became adept in turning Samoan phrases in proper style. He was 'Le Ona', the rich proprietor, and those Samoans who considered themselves under his protection called themselves 'Tama Ona', which Louis rendered for Colvin as 'the MacRichies'; he thought of their relationship to him as that of members of a Highland clan to their chief. He was also 'Tusitala', which Louis explained to Colvin meant literally 'Chief White Information'. The Samoans, incidentally, had no conception of fiction as an imaginative art and considered Louis's role of story-teller as that of purveyor of fact. When he wrote 'The Bottle Imp' for a Polynesian audience, and had it serialized in a Samoan translation in a missionary paper, he found that it led to a general belief that he really did possess a magic bottle with a demon inside who would give him whatever he wanted. Something of his reputation for a command of magical powers rubbed off on Fanny and on his mother, and sometimes proved helpful in managing the servants.

Fanny looked after the planting, and experimented with a variety of crops, while Belle was housekeeper and general manager indoors (later she became Louis's amanuensis and wrote to his dictation). Louis rode down to Apia on horseback on business or pleasure, involved himself in local politics, and presided over his clan with a growing sense of responsibility for their moral welfare. The little boy who had played at being a minister and the young man who had fiercely formulated his ethical views in opposition to conventional bourgeois Christianity now in his early forties sought to develop a simple moral and religious code which could be presented in intelligible terms without offending traditional views. The result was family prayers at Vailima, posthumously published as *Vailima Prayers*. In July 1894, having heard that his Bournemouth friend Adelaide Boodle was going into mission work, he wrote to her giving advice he had learned from experience. 'Forget wholly and for ever all small pruderies, and remember that *you cannot change ancestral feelings of right and wrong without what is practically soul murder*. Barbarous as the customs may seem, always hear them with patience, always judge them with gentleness, always find in them some seed of good; see that you always develop them; remember that all you can do is to civilize the man in the line of his own civilization, such as it is.' Anthropologists today recognize the wisdom of this advice, ignored by so many nineteenth-century missionaries with unhappy social and cultural consequences.

Samoan politics were complicated by the impact of the interests of three Powers – Germany, Britain and the United States – on a traditional system of native kingship and chieftainship based on an orally transmitted complex of ideas about the kinds of prestige attached to certain titles and names. Louis distrusted the three-Power involvement in Samoa, since it led to the backing by different powers of rival puppet kings with consequent loss of Samoan dignity and social harmony. He objected to the strong German influence, and believed that Britain should show some real responsibility for the social welfare and efficient government of the islands. *A Footnote to History* shows that he had really mastered the strange facts of Samoan political history. Among

Tortoiseshell ring, with the name 'Tusitala' inlaid in silver, belonging to Louis.

Samoan chief: watercolour by G. Pieri Nerli.

94

Samoan Chief

233

the rival chiefs he was on the side of the ablest, Mataafa, who was distrusted by the British missions as being a Roman Catholic, while the Germans supported his kinsman Malietoa and the Foreign Office saw no reason to start a quarrel with Germany over Samoan affairs when they had other fish to fry. In July 1893 Mataafa led a rebellion against the German-installed Malietoa, and this ended with Mataafa's exile to the Marshall Islands, though not before Louis and his friends had given his forces such help as they could. Many of Mataafa's supporters were imprisoned in Apia gaol, and Louis, with Fanny, Belle and Lloyd, openly visited them with gifts and in return were guests of honour at a feast given by the prisoners in the prison courtyard. There was something of the comic opera – as Louis pointed out – in much of this, but the human issues were real, and Louis's main concern was with the welfare of the natives and the preservation of their dignity and self-respect. His interventions, in the form of letters to the Press and in more concrete ways, irritated both German and British officials. But Louis continued to act as he thought right. In the end he protested that he could 'see but one way out', namely that the three Powers withdraw 'and the natives be let alone, and allowed to govern the islands as they choose'. In September 1894 a number of chiefs who had been imprisoned after Mataafa's rebellion and had now been released offered, as a token of their gratitude for all that Louis had done for them, to make him a new road from the main track across the island to Vailima. They kept their promise, and when the road was finished Louis held a great celebratory feast for the chiefs, at which he read a speech in Samoan (a missionary had done the translation for him) of high formality and moral advice. The names of twenty-two chiefs appear below the inscription on the signpost which they erected at the entrance to the road, which said that the road was an expression of their gratitude for 'the surpassing kindness of Mr R. L. Stevenson and his loving care during our tribulations while in prison'.

The road to Vailima (called by the Samoan chiefs who built it Ala Loto Alofa, the 'Road of the Loving Heart'): watercolour by G. Pieri Nerli.

The feast held by Louis (at the head of the table, with Fanny) to celebrate the completion of the Road of the Loving Heart.

That was in the late autumn of 1894. Early in the previous year he had paid a visit to Australia and, though once again he was largely confined to his room in Sydney, he spent some weeks there with considerable satisfaction, for he could now see plainly how widespread his high reputation was: he was besieged by distinguished visitors. In September 1893, shortly after the defeat of Mataafa's rebellion, he visited Honolulu, chiefly for the sake of the voyage, intending to return by the next steamer. But he developed pneumonia at his boarding-house in Waikiki and Fanny had to come out from Samoa to bring him home. He never left Samoa again. Although he had two or three slight haemorrhages during the whole of his stay there and had other bouts of relatively minor illness he was able to lead a normal and indeed an extremely active life. The climate clearly agreed with him. If tuberculosis was indeed what he had, then it had now been arrested.

Recent research, especially study of the passages in Louis's letters that were suppressed by Colvin in his edition of them, has however revealed that the last two years of Louis's life were much disturbed by worry about Fanny's instability and by the behaviour of other members of his 'clan'. Bradford Booth has attributed the fact that in the last years Louis worked on four novels inter-mittently and interchangeably, without being able to finish any of them, to 'Fanny's abnormal behaviour', 'which seriously interfered with Louis's creativity'. Lloyd was having an affair with a native girl that deeply distressed his mother, and Belle could behave impulsively and aggressively. It may be that the cost of preserving his life and relative health for a few more years – if this can indeed be attributed to his stay in the South Seas – was too heavy, and that the sense of isolation together with increasing domestic worries impaired his maturing creative gifts.

This may help to explain why, for all his involvement in Samoan affairs, Louis was aware of himself as an exile and his imagination dwelt more and more in Scotland. In October 1891 he had written to Henry James that his

Fanny with a Samoan girl.

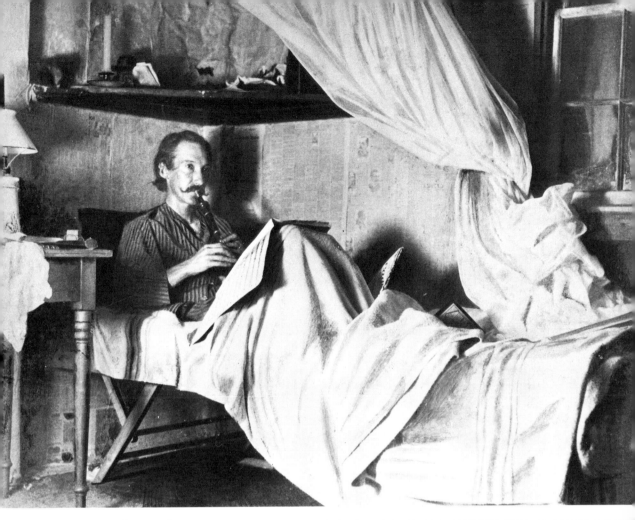

Louis in bed, playing his flageolet.

Pen drawing by Louis of the harbour
entrance at Waikiki beach, by
Diamond Head.

Diamond Head & Waikiki beach. Entrance of the Harbor

sequel to *Kidnapped* 'is on the stocks at last'. It was finished the following year, and first published serially in *Atalanta* in 1892–93 under the title *David Balfour*. (This has remained its American title, while in Britain it has always been known as *Catriona*.) It is a different kind of novel from *Kidnapped*, and its first part shows a kind of emotional involvement a clue to which is found in his dedication to Charles Baxter:

There should be left in our native city some seed of the elect; some long-legged, hot-headed youth must repeat to-day our dreams and wanderings of so many years ago; he will relish the pleasure, which should have been ours, to follow among named streets and numbered houses the country walks of David Balfour, to identify Dean, and Silvermills, and Broughton, and Hope Park and Pilrig, and poor old Lochend – if it still be standing, and the Figgate Whins – if there be any of them left; or to push (on a long holiday) so far afield as Gillane or the Bass. . . .

You are still . . . in the venerable city which I must always think of as my home. And I have come so far; and the sights and thoughts of my youth pursue me; and I see like a vision the youth of my father, and of his father, and the whole stream of lives flowing down there, far in the north, with the sound of laughter and tears, to cast me out in the end, as by a sudden freshet, on these ultimate islands. And I admire and bow my head before the romance of destiny.

The Stevensonian topographical element in the first part of *Catriona* is less the fitting of action to physical setting, which had earlier been his aim, than an attempt to reincarnate a possible earlier self of his in a known historical situation and a well-remembered landscape.

> *Sing me a song of a lad that is gone,*
> *Say, could that lad be I?*

Louis wrote in his original version of the 'Skye Boat Song', and we feel that the question is also posed in this novel. There is a note of self-pity qualifying the heroism that intrigues the reader in the earlier chapters. It is not a flaw, for it is realized with considerable psychological subtlety and total conviction. Only later, when David goes to Holland and lives in a peculiar brother-and-sister relationship with Catriona, does Stevenson appear to be backing away from something he cannot or will not look at closely. The portrait of Catriona's father is in his best vein with plausible scoundrels – and it took some courage to paint the heroine's father in this way – but the girls in the novel are not, as it were, telling the whole truth. Barbara Grant is much more interesting than Catriona, and she plays an important and convincing part in the first and finer part of the novel. But Louis has to drop her when he takes David from Scotland to Holland and changes him from a morally interesting hero, trying in vain to give evidence at a rigged court that will save an innocent life, to a passive victim of circumstance. The biographer of Stevenson cannot avoid the suspicion that in some indirect and unconscious way the presence in the background of Fanny prevented him from following through his quasi-biographical insights into fully realized renderings of his hero's relations with women. If this is so, he was to overcome the inhibition in his unfinished masterpiece *Weir of Hermiston*.

Nevertheless, the first part of *Catriona* can stand as a splendid short novel on its own, showing an absolute assurance in the handling of character and incident and a style of quiet maturity capable of a great range of tones. Maturity of a different kind is shown in *The Ebb-Tide* (inspired by the South Seas this time, not Scotland), a story in which Lloyd helped with the plot but of which the final writing is clearly all Louis's. 'My dear man,' he wrote to James in June 1893, 'the grimness of that story is not to be depicted in words. There are only four characters, to be sure, but they are such a troop of swine!' *The Ebb-Tide*, first serialized in 1893–94 and published in book form in 1894, is a powerful story set with great physical vividness and precision in its South Seas environment, in which different kinds and degrees of evil are set against each other with remarkable dramatic effect. Its closest parallel in Stevenson's work is the more or less contemporary story *The Beach of Falesá*, the first and by far the most important story in *Island Nights' Entertainment*, published in 1893.

Illustration from 'The Bottle Imp', one of the stories in *Island Nights' Entertainment* (first edition).

On the surface a picturesque local-colour story, based on the author's know-ledge of the South Seas, with a contrived happy ending, *The Beach of Falesá* is essentially a finely devised ironic comment on the double moral standard that obtains when the white man imposes his culture (or part of it) on a more primitive civilization. The good-natured insensitivity of the narrator, who does not understand the moral implications of his own attitude or his own story, is implicitly contrasted with what the story itself says, and the result is a tale which combines power and subtlety in a positively Jamesian way. James himself thought so. 'The art of *The Beach of Falesá*,' he wrote to Louis, 'seems to me an art brought to a perfection and I delight in the observed truth, the modesty of nature, of the narrator.'

Louis in Samoa. Painting by G. Pieri Nerli.

Louis's desk at Vailima.

Louis dictating to Belle Strong, 1892.

103

Louis's custom was to have several books going at the same time, and to leave off work on one and start work on another as the spirit moved him. On 1 November 1892 he wrote to J. M. Barrie: 'I have just finished *David Balfour*; I have another book on the stocks, *The Young Chevalier*, which is to be part in France and part in Scotland, and to deal with Prince Charlie about the year 1749; and now what have I done but begun a third which is to be all moor-land together, and is to have for a centrepiece a figure that I think you will appreciate – that of the immortal Braxfield.' He never got very far with *The Young Chevalier* or with some other novels he began in 1893. The Braxfield story was the unfinished *Weir of Hermiston*. He had been working on it for several months when he began, in a very different mood and vein, *St Ives*, which was also left unfinished at his death.

St Ives is a picaresque adventure story which seems at first sight to belong to an earlier phase of Stevenson's career. But it is also a symbolic searching for the author's early self. Its hero is an English-speaking Frenchman, a prisoner of war in Edinburgh Castle during the Napoleonic wars, who falls in love with an Edinburgh girl, escapes, has adventures, and was certainly meant to win through to a happy ending. The novel is full of Louis's Edinburgh memories. St Ives, his hero, sees the lamplighter hurrying along the Edin-burgh streets at dusk just as little Louis had, as he recalled in the well-known verses in *A Child's Garden*; he roams the city streets at night and takes part in bohemian adventures as Louis and Charles Baxter and Bob Stevenson had done; and the girl he loves lives in the very Swanston cottage where Louis had spent so many happy summers. The bohemian Frenchman in Edinburgh is a rendering of Louis in his student days: he is made French to symbolize his difference from the respectable citizens of the city, and he is first presented to us as a prisoner as though to symbolize the imprisoning effect of the bourgeois conventions against which Louis had so fiercely rebelled. Yet it was not a book that Louis took seriously. He wrote Bob a long letter in 1894 giving him the results of his inquiries into their common ancestry and then reporting on work in progress. '. . . The present book, *Saint Ives*, is nothing; it is in no style in particular, a tissue of adventures, the central character is not very well done, no philosophic pith under the yarn; and, in short, if people will read it, that's all I ask; and if they won't, damn them!' He had come to 'a crossing place', and what he was crossing to was represented not by this novel but by *Weir of Hermiston*. This was the novel on which he was solely engaged during the weeks preceding his death.

'It is a singular thing,' Louis wrote to Barrie in the letter already quoted, 'that I should live here in the South Seas under conditions so new and so striking, and yet my imagination so continually inhabit that cold old huddle of grey hills from which we come.' In writing *Weir of Hermiston* his imagina-tion inhabited the Pentland Hills and the Lammermuirs and, further, the whole of the Scottish Border country where his Elliot ancestors had 'shaken a spear in the Debateable land' and the balladists had recorded the tragic destinies of fighting men and lovers. It dwelt also in Edinburgh, where the first part of the novel is set, and it dwelt with a kind of loving repulsion on the character of Lord Braxfield, scourge of the radicals in the Edinburgh

Some of the Scottish scenery which formed the setting of *Weir of Hermiston*: the Lammermuir Hills, East Lothian, seen from Dirleton Castle.

miss me?" He battled —

cried in a doubled voice.

The doctor turned about and looked him all over with a clinical eye. The young man's whole attitude smelt of domestic discord; a far more stupid man than Dr. Gregory must have divined the truth, but ninety-nine men out of a hundred, even if they had been equally inclined to charity, would have blundered by some touch of charitable exaggeration. The doctor was better inspired. After a moment's pause, he told the truth —

Kindness

"Well, I'll tell you why," said he — "It was when you had the measles, Mr. Archibald, you had them bad and ill; and I thought you were going to slip between my fingers. The day came when there was a change, and I went down to announce it to your father. 'There is a change, Hermiston,' said I. He said nothing, but glowered at me (if you'll excuse me) like a wild beast. 'A change for the better,' said I. Well, I heard him take his breath."

And the doctor, leaving no opportunity for any anticlimax, made his escape.

Raeburn's portrait of Lord Braxfield, on whom Louis based the character of Weir of Hermiston. 'If I know gusto when I see it, this canvas was painted with rare enjoyment. . . . A peculiarly subtle expression haunts the lower part, sensual and incredulous, like that of a man tasting good Bordeaux with half a fancy that it has been somewhat too long uncorked.' ('Some Portraits by Raeburn', essay in *Virginibus Puerisque*.)

Page from Louis's autograph manuscript of *Weir of Hermiston*.

political trials of the 1790s (when fear of the influence of the French Revolution provoked fierce government action against the mildest reformers), brutal, sensual, coarsely witty in speech, yet a man of honour and integrity in his own way. Louis had been fascinated by Braxfield ever since as a young man he had seen Raeburn's portrait of him exhibited in the Royal Scottish Academy. This sent him to Lord Cockburn's hostile account in his *Memorials*, and he drew on both Raeburn and Cockburn for the account of Braxfield included in his essay 'Some Portraits by Raeburn' which had appeared in *Virginibus Puerisque* in 1881. 'He was the last judge on the Scottish bench to employ the pure Scottish idiom,' Louis had written. 'His opinions, thus given in Doric, and conceived in a lively, rugged, conversational style, were full of point and authority. Out of the bar, or off the bench, he was a convivial man, a lover of wine, and one who "shone peculiarly" at tavern meetings. He left behind him an unrivalled reputation for rough and cruel speech; and to this day his name smacks of the gallows.' Give such a man an idealistic and sensitive son and you could achieve a classic conflict of opposed characters and ideals. Set the story of such a conflict partly in Edinburgh and partly in the Scottish Border country and it could be related to a sense both of history and of topography. Introduce an element of sex, with timid innocence and confident sophistication involved with the same simple-hearted country girl, and you get a new moral dimension. Have this involve the idealistic young man in murder of his sophisticated rival for seducing the girl he himself loved innocently, and have him tried before his own father the judge, and you have a blow-up to staggering proportions of the father-son conflict that had haunted

Stevenson since his student days. Stevenson's Lord Justice-Clerk, Weir of Hermiston, was based on Braxfield; he is portrayed in the novel as judge, as husband and as father before the novel widens its scope to include the 'cold old huddle of grey hills' that Louis kept brooding on in exile. Though he never finished the novel, he completed the dedicatory verses; they were addressed to his wife, and in them he tried to persuade her to share his vision of his well-remembered Scotland:

> *I saw rain falling and the rainbow drawn*
> *On Lammermuir. Hearkening I heard again*
> *In my precipitous city beaten bells*
> *Winnow the keen sea wind. And here afar,*
> *Intent on my own race and place, I wrote. . . .*

On 17 May 1893 Louis wrote to S. R. Crockett: 'I shall never take that walk by the Fisher's Tryst and Glencorse. I shall never see Auld Reekie. I shall never set my foot again upon the heather. Here I am until I die, and here will I be buried. The word is out and the doom written.' In the same letter he wrote: '*Weir of Hermiston* is a much greater undertaking [than *The Ebb-Tide*], and the plot is not good, I fear; but Lord Justice Clerk Hermiston ought to be a plum.' The basic plot was in fact splendid, but Louis was planning to avoid a tragic ending, and he felt uneasy about it. The whole texture of the novel as written is tragic, and Louis knew it. In his letter to Barrie of November 1892 he told him that Barrie's novel *The Little Minister* 'ought to have ended badly; we all know it did'; and then gave the contrary instance of Meredith's *The Ordeal of Richard Feverel*, which 'begins to end well; and then tricks you and ends ill'. He then goes on to discuss the ending of his 'Braxfield story', admitting that it is 'a heavy case of conscience'. 'Braxfield – only his name is Hermiston – has a son who is condemned to death; plainly, there is a fine tempting fitness about this; and I meant he was to hang. But now on considering my minor characters, I saw there were five people who would – in a sense who must – break prison and attempt his rescue. They were capable, hardy folks, too, who might very well succeed. Why should they not then? Why should not young Hermiston escape clear out of the country?' But he knew why not, and the critic may well feel that if Louis had lived to finish the novel he might have betrayed his instincts as an artist. He had had trouble before, with the ending of *The Master of Ballantrae*, but this was more serious.

As it is, *Weir of Hermiston* is a magnificent fragment. The writing is simultaneously taut and eloquent. The use of Scots in the mouth of Hermiston in the great confrontation with his son – Archie's clipped English vowels and studiously genteel vocabulary contrasting with his father's broad Scots vowels and calculated brutality of speech – is the finest thing of its kind in Scottish literature. The change in tone when he moves from a city to a country environment shows Stevenson putting his topographical sense most memorably at the service of his sense of human character and destiny. He was a mature novelist at the height of his powers on that morning of 3 December 1894 when he worked in full inspiration at chapter nine of *Weir*. He left off in the afternoon to answer some letters. Then, at sunset, he came downstairs to tease

Fanny about the sense of foreboding she could not shake off. They played cards together to cheer her up. He went down to the cellar to bring up a bottle of Burgundy for dinner, then went out on the veranda to Fanny, 'gaily talking', as Lloyd remembered, 'when suddenly he put both hands to his head, and cried out, "What's that?" Then he asked quickly, "Do I look strange?" Even as he did so he fell on his knees beside her.' They helped him on to a chair, unconscious, and then laid him on a bed, but he never recovered consciousness. He died that evening at ten minutes past eight.

Louis lying in state.

109

The road to his grave was cut with knives and axes up the steep face of Mount Vaea by forty chiefs, who knew that Tusitala had wanted to be buried on the summit and showed their love for him by making this possible. They were at work by dawn the next day, and at one o'clock in the afternoon a party of Samoans carried the coffin, covered with the red ensign from the *Casco*, to the top of the mountain where Samoans had also dug the grave. Later, a concrete slab was erected on the level grave, with two bronze plaques, the eastern one carrying the well-known verses from Stevenson's 'Requiem', concluding

> *Here he lies where he longed to be;*
> *Home is the sailor, home from sea,*
> *And the hunter home from the hill.*

He could not have known where the 'here' would be, when he wrote those verses, years before. On the last day of his life his imagination inhabited Scotland. He was above all a Scottish novelist, as Scottish in his way as Walter Scott, whose imagination was also nurtured on the townscape and countryside of his native land. His skills as romancer, essayist, writer of adventure stories, historical novelist, analyst of the moral ambiguities of the human animal, were slow to come together in his work, but they were coming together in his later writing with a new kind of maturity. Above all, his Calvinist ancestors and his artistic bohemianism, working together in counterpoint, kept fertilizing his imagination. Henley once described him in a sonnet ('R.L.S.') which ended

Louis' tomb at the summit of Mount Vaea. (*Opposite*) One of the plaques on the tomb is inscribed with verses from Louis' poem 'Requiem'. The penultimate line has been misquoted as 'Home is the sailor, home from the sea'.

Most vain, most generous, sternly critical,
Buffoon and poet, lover and sensualist:
A deal of Ariel, just a streak of Puck,
Much Antony, of Hamlet most of all,
And something of the Shorter-Catechist.

The modern critic and biographer finds no cause to quarrel with this description. He would emphasize, perhaps, the 'most generous', for even the offended and offending Henley was the recipient of financial help from Louis, who supported a large clan and in addition was continually helping his friends with money – he once wrote to Baxter (who had charge of his finances) to help Colvin if he was in trouble even if it meant ruining him (Louis).

He was famous and reasonably rich in his last years, something of a legend in his distant South Seas hideaway. News of his sudden death produced an enormous shock-wave across Europe and America. Henry James at first refused to believe the news. 'It isn't *true*, it isn't *true*, say it isn't true,' he cried to Mrs Sitwell, and he wrote to Gosse, 'Of what can one think or utter or dream, save of this ghastly extinction of the beloved R.L.S.?' But he later wrote that Louis 'met his end in the happiest form, by the straight, swift bolt of the gods'. In this same essay, a review of Louis's letters first published in the January 1900 issue of *The North American Review*, James talked of the Stevenson legend. 'It has been his fortune (whether or no the greatest that can befall a man of letters) to have had to consent to become, by a process not purely mystic and not wholly untraceable – what shall we call it? – a Figure. . . . This case of the figure is of the rarest, and the honour surely of the greatest.

In all our literature we can count them, sometimes with the work and some-times without. The work has often been great and yet the figure *nil*. Johnson was one, and Goldsmith and Byron; and the two former, moreover, not in any degree, like Stevenson, in virtue of the element of grace.' Since James wrote, the Figure first displaced the writer, then was deliberately disfigured, and then was restored to common humanity. But the Figure remains. It is not the 'Seraph in Chocolate' that Henley objected to, nor yet the heroically optimistic invalid of early twentieth-century legend. What sometimes looked like optimism was really a wryly pragmatic acceptance of the inexplicable contradictions of life and the inevitability of extinction at death. The Figure remains because it embodies something central both in modern literature and in modern personality – a sense of endurance combined with a relish of experience; a humorous enjoyment of human nature together with an awareness of society's oppressive conventions; an authentic personal know-ledge of the nightmarish quality of the lives of men trapped in their own natures and their physical environments qualified by a belief that men could by will-power define their own moral world; a deep love of one's own place and a desire to find roots, together with a commitment to exile. On top of all this, and most important of all for the persistence of the Figure, Robert Louis Stevenson was an enchanting personality: anyone who has lived for some time with his letters as well as his novels and stories and essays, and who knows, too, the Scottish background which always meant so much to him, feels a kind of understanding, an affection even, which is for the man as much as for the artist.

View of Apia today.

Map showing Louis's life and travels in the South Seas. The broken line indicates his voyages on board the *Janet Nicoll*.

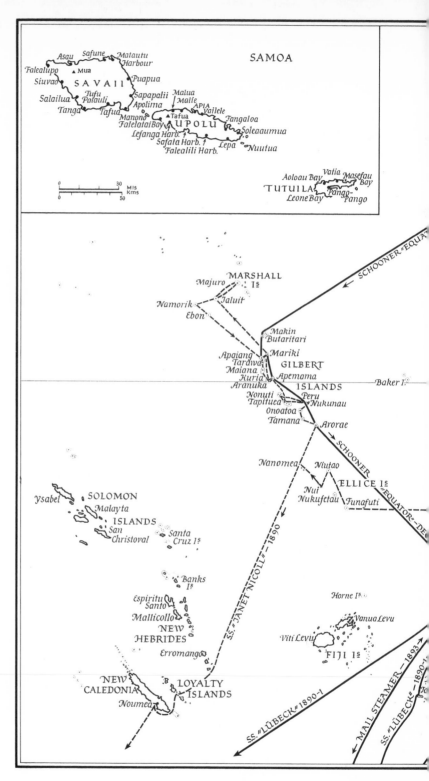

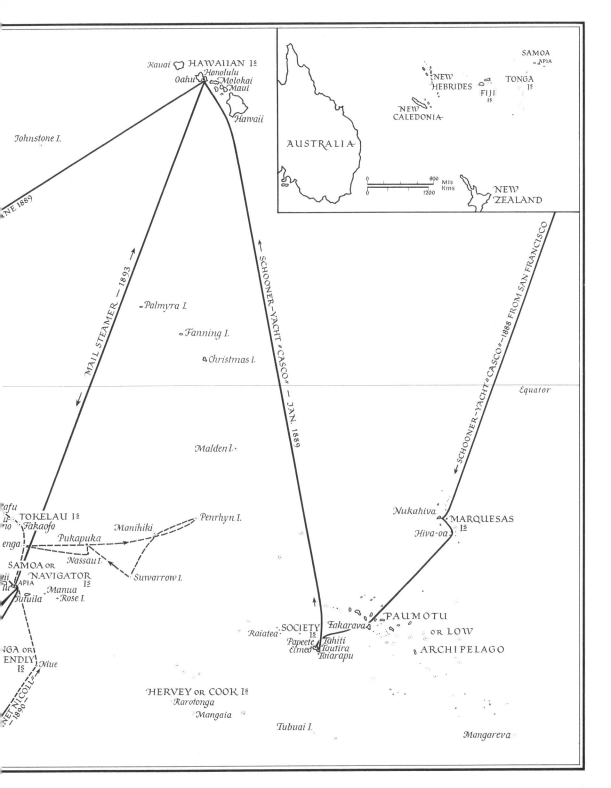

Kauai HAWAIIAN Iˢ
Oahu Honolulu
Molokai
Maui
Hawaii

Johnstone I.

NE 1889

SAMOA
APIA
NEW
HEBRIDES
TONGA
Iˢ
FIJI
Iˢ
NEW
CALEDONIA

AUSTRALIA

800 Mis
1200 Kms

NEW
ZEALAND

MAIL STEAMER — 1893

SCHOONER-YACHT "CASCO" — JAN. 1889

SCHOONER-YACHT "CASCO"—1888 FROM SAN FRANCISCO

Palmyra I.

Fanning I.

Christmas I.

Equator

Malden I.

Nukahiva MARQUESAS
Iˢ
Hiva-oa

afu
i
no Fakaofo TOKELAU Iˢ
enga
Pukapuka Manihiki
Nassau I.
SAMOA or
NAVIGATOR Iˢ
APIA
lu Manua
Tutuila Rose I.
Suwarrow I.

Penrhyn I.

NGA or
ENDLY Iˢ Niue

NET NICOLL
1890

HERVEY or COOK Iˢ
Rarotonga
Mangaia

Tubuai I.

Raiatea SOCIETY
Iˢ
Papeete Tahiti
Eimeo Tautira
Taiarapu

Fakarava
PAUMOTU
or LOW
ARCHIPELAGO

Mangareva

115

ROBERT·LOVIS·STEVENSON·

1850 13 November: Stevenson born at Edinburgh

1867 November: enters Edinburgh University

1868 July–September: visits harbour works in Anstruther and Wick

1869 March: elected to the Speculative Society

1871 April: gives up engineering for law

1873 January: first crisis with his parents. July: meets Mrs Sitwell and Sidney Colvin. November: goes to Menton for his health, remaining till the following April

1874 June: elected to Savile Club, which becomes his London headquarters. November: resumes law classes at Edinburgh University

1875 February: meets W. E. Henley at Edinburgh Infirmary. July: admitted to the Scottish Bar. In France with Bob Stevenson. Meets Mrs Fanny Van de Grift Osbourne

1876 August–October: canoe trip with Sir Walter Simpson on the Continent

1877 Early summer: at Grez. September: at Paris with Fanny Osbourne

1878 May: publication of *An Inland Voyage*. August: Fanny Osbourne returns to America. September–October: walking tour with donkey in the Cévannes. December: publication of *Edinburgh: Picturesque Notes*

1879 June: publication of *Travels with a Donkey*. 7 August: sails for America. September–December: in Monterey, California, with Fanny and her family

1880 19 May: married to Fanny in San Francisco. August: returns to Scotland, with Fanny and Lloyd Osbourne. Reconciliation with parents. November: to Davos, Switzerland, where they stay until the following April

1881 June–July: in Pitlochry, Scotland. August–September: in Braemar. Begins *The Sea-Cook* (*Treasure Island*). October: returns to Davos, staying until the following April

1882 March: publication of *Familar Studies of Men and Books*. June–August: in Scotland. September: goes to South of France for his health. October: settles in Campagne Defli, near Marseilles

1883 March: settles in the Chalet 'La Solitude', Hyères. December: publication of *Treasure Island*

1884 Summer: driven from 'La Solitude' by cholera and returns to England. September: they settle in Bournemouth

1885 March: publication of *A Child's Garden of Verses*. April: the Stevensons settle in their new Bournemouth house, 'Skerryvore'

1886 January: publication of *Dr Jekyll and Mr Hyde*. July: publication of *Kidnapped*

1887 August: leaves Britain for good. October: settles at Saranac

1888 March: quarrel with Henley. 28 June: sets out from San Francisco on his first South Seas voyage

1889 September: publication of *The Master of Ballantrae*. December: in Samoa. Buys 'Vailima', estate in Upolu

1890 February: in Sydney, Australia. April–August: cruise aboard the *Janet Nicoll* to Gilbert, Marshall and other islands. August–September: in Sydney. October: settles at 'Vailima'

1893 February: in Sydney. September: publication of *David Balfour* (*Catriona*)

1894 3 December: death at 'Vailima'

SELECT BIBLIOGRAPHY

Janet Adam Smith, ed., *Henry James and Robert Louis Stevenson: A Record of Friendship and Criticism* (London, 1948)

Janet Adam Smith, ed., *Robert Louis Stevenson: Collected Poems*, with Introduction and Notes (2nd edition, London, 1971)

Graham Balfour, *The Life of Robert Louis Stevenson* (2 vols, London, 1901)

Bradford A. Booth, 'The Vailima Letters of Robert Louis Stevenson', *Harvard Library Bulletin*, vol. XV, no. 2 (April 1967)

Sidney Colvin, ed., *The Letters of Stevenson to his Family and Friends* (4 vols, London, 1911)

DeLancey Ferguson and Marshall Waingrow, ed., *R.L.S.: Stevenson's Letters to Charles Baxter* (New Haven, Connecticut, 1956)

J. C. Furnas, *Voyage to Windward: the Life of Robert Louis Stevenson* (New York, 1951; London, 1952)

J. D. Hart, ed., *From Scotland to Silverado* (Cambridge, Massachusetts, 1966). (Contains in their entirety all of Stevenson's previously published and unpublished writings about his journey to California in 1879–80.)

Anne Roller Issler, *Happier for his Presence: San Francisco and Robert Louis Stevenson* [Stanford, 1949]

G. L. McKay, ed., *The Stevenson Library of E. J. Beinecke* (6 vols, New Haven, Connecticut, 1951–64)

Rosaline Masson, *The Life of Robert Louis Stevenson* (London, 1923)

W. F. Prideaux, *A Bibliography of the Works of Robert Louis Stevenson*, new and revised edition edited and supplemented by Mrs Luther S. Livingston (London, 1918)

Robert Louis Stevenson, *Records of a Family of Engineers* (London, 1912)

Robert Louis Stevenson, *Memories and Portraits* (London, 1887)

There have been many collected editions of Stevenson's works, including the following:

Edinburgh Edition, ed. Sidney Colvin (28 vols, 1894–98)

Thistle Edition (26 vols, 1902)

Pentland Edition, ed. Edmund Gosse (20 vols, 1906–7)

Vailima Edition, ed. Lloyd Osbourne and F. Van de G. Stevenson (26 vols, 1922–23)

Tusitala Edition (35 vols, 1923–24)

South Seas Edition (32 vols, 1925)

Cunningham. Lady Stair's House Museum, Edinburgh.

Robert Louis Stevenson, aged about ten, riding a donkey. Lady Stair's House Museum, Edinburgh.

21 Coast near Wick, Caithness. Photo British Tourist Authority.

22 Page from a letter from Robert Louis Stevenson to his mother, with a drawing of North Uist Lighthouse, 18 June 1869. The Beinecke Rare Book and Manuscript Library, Yale University.

23 Sir Walter Simpson. Photograph from Eve B. Simpson, *The Robert Louis Stevenson Originals* (1912). British Museum, London.

24 Robert Louis Stevenson in costume for *Deianira*, 1877. Lady Stair's House Museum, Edinburgh.

25 Thomas Stevenson. Oil-painting by George Reid. Scottish National Portrait Gallery, Edinburgh. Photo National Galleries of Scotland.

29 Page from a letter from Robert Louis Stevenson to Mrs Sitwell, Siron's Inn, Barbizon, 1875. Trustees of the National Library of Scotland, Edinburgh.

31 Menton. French Government Tourist Office.

33 Sidney Colvin. Photograph by J. Russell and Sons. British Museum, London, Department of Prints and Drawings.

34 Robert Louis Stevenson as Barrister-at-Law, 1875. Lady Stair's House Museum, Edinburgh.

37 Siron's Inn, Barbizon, *c.* 1875. Lady Stair's House Museum, Edinburgh.

Street in Fontainebleau. Engraving (*Millet's House*) from Robert Louis Stevenson, 'Fontainebleau', in *Magazine of Art*, 1884. British Museum, London.

38 The bridge at Grez. Oil-painting by Fanny Osbourne, *c.* 1875. Lady Stair's House Museum, Edinburgh.

40 Samuel C. Osbourne. Silverado Museum, St Helena, California.

41 Fanny Osbourne. The Beinecke Rare Book and Manuscript Library, Yale University.

Virginia City. Lithograph by C. C. Kuchel after Grafton T. Brown, 1861. Library of Congress, Washington.

42 Frontispiece by Walter Crane from Robert Louis Stevenson, *An Inland Voyage* (1878). British Museum, London.

43 Frontispiece by Walter Crane from Robert Louis Stevenson, *Travels with a Donkey* (1879). British Museum, London.

Robert Louis Stevenson aged twenty-six. Etching after Fanny Stevenson. Mansell Collection.

45 10 West Street, New York. Photograph from John A. Hammerton,

Stevensoniana (1910). British Museum, London.

46 Scene at a station on the Union Pacific Railway. Engraving from *Frank Leslie's Illustrated Newspaper*, 11 December 1869. Library of Congress, Washington.

47 Alvarado Street, Monterey, 1875. Monterey State Department of Parks and Recreation.

48 The house in Monterey where Robert Louis Stevenson lived in 1879. Lady Stair's House Museum, Edinburgh.

50 Record of the marriage of Robert Louis Stevenson and Fanny Osbourne, 19 May 1880. Reproduced by permission of the Director of the Bancroft Library.

51 Frontispiece by Joe Strong from Robert Louis Stevenson, *The Silverado Squatters* (volume III in Stevenson's *Works*, 1894–98). British Museum, London.

52 John Addington Symonds. Chalk-drawing by Carlo Orsi. National Portrait Gallery, London.

53 Davos, Switzerland. Watercolour by Mrs Ruck-Keene, 1882–83. Lady Stair's House Museum, Edinburgh.

54 'The Cottage', Braemar. Lady Stair's House Museum, Edinburgh.

56 Illustration from Robert Louis Stevenson, *Treasure Island*, serialized in *Young Folks*, July 1881 to June 1882. Lady Stair's House Museum, Edinburgh.

57 Frontispiece of Robert Louis Stevenson, *Treasure Island* (1883). British Museum, London.

58 Advertisement at the end of Robert Louis Stevenson, *Moral Emblems* (1882). British Museum, London.

'The Careful Angler'. Woodcut from Robert Louis Stevenson, *Moral Emblems* (1882). British Museum, London.

59 Kingussie. Photo Edwin Smith.

60 Edmund Gosse. Oil-painting by John Singer Sargent, 1886. National Portrait Gallery, London.

61 Page from Robert Louis Stevenson, *A Child's Garden of Verses* (1896). British Museum, London.

Illustration from Robert Louis Stevenson, *The Black Arrow* (1888). British Museum, London.

62 Robert Louis and Fanny Stevenson. Oil-painting by John Singer Sargent, 1885. From the collection of Mr and Mrs John Hay Whitney.

63 'Skerryvore'. Etching by Leslie M. Ward, 1912, from *The Bookman*, 1913. British Museum, London.

64 Bournemouth, *c.* 1880s. Radio Times Hulton Picture Library.

65 Henry James. Photograph by Hoppé. Mansell Collection.

67 Pen and ink drawing by William Boucher for Robert Louis Stevenson, *Kidnapped*, serialized in *Young Folks*, 1886. Lady Stair's House Museum, Edinburgh.

68 William Archer. Photograph by Barraud. British Museum, London, Department of Prints and Drawings.

71 Robert Louis and Fanny Stevenson with Lloyd Osbourne on the veranda of the cottage at Saranac Lake, winter 1887–88. Lady Stair's House Museum, Edinburgh.

72 Robert Louis Stevenson. Statue in bronzed plaster by D. W. Stevenson. Glasgow Art Gallery and Museum.

73 Robert Louis Stevenson. Bronze plaque by Augustus Saint Gaudens, 1887. Jardins du Luxembourg, Paris. Photo Giraudon.

75 Page from the original typescript of Lloyd Osbourne, *The Wrong Box*, with handwritten corrections by Robert Louis Stevenson, *c.* 1889. The Beinecke Rare Book and Manuscript Library, Yale University.

Lloyd Osbourne. Lady Stair's House Museum, Edinburgh.

76 W. E. Henley. Photograph by F. Hollyer. Radio Times Hulton Picture Library.

77 Katherine de Mattos. Anonymous watercolour. Lady Stair's House Museum, Edinburgh.

79 The schooner *Casco*. Lady Stair's House Museum, Edinburgh.

82 Lloyd Osbourne, Fanny and Robert Louis Stevenson, King Kalakaua and Mrs Thomas Stevenson in the cabin of the *Casco*. Lady Stair's House Museum, Edinburgh.

83 The church at the old leper settlement on the island of Molokai. Edinburgh Public Libraries.

85 Samoan girl. Watercolour by Joe Strong, 1891. Silverado Museum, St Helena, California.

86 *The Cutter's Deck.* Pencil sketch by Robert Louis Stevenson. Edinburgh Public Libraries.

Robert Louis Stevenson on the bowsprit of the *Equator*. Lady Stair's House Museum, Edinburgh.

87 Apia, Samoa, at the end of the nineteenth century. Edinburgh Public Libraries.

King Tembinok' and his entourage leaving the *Janet Nicoll* at the island of Apemama. Photograph from Lloyd Osbourne's album. Lady Stair's House Museum, Edinburgh.

90 Robert Louis Stevenson. Lady Stair's House Museum, Edinburgh.

Baptismal font made from a coconut. Lady Stair's House Museum, Edinburgh.

91 Robert Louis Stevenson, with his family and household, outside Vailima, 31 July 1892. Lady Stair's House Museum, Edinburgh.

92 The interior of Vailima. Engraving. Mansell Collection.

93 Vailima. Wash drawing by Belle Strong, 22 June 1891. Lady Stair's House Museum, Edinburgh.

94 Tortoiseshell ring, with the name 'Tusitala' inlaid in silver, belonging to Robert Louis Stevenson. Lady Stair's House Museum, Edinburgh.

95 Samoan chief. Watercolour by G. Pieri Nerli, 1892. Lady Stair's House Museum, Edinburgh.

96 The Road of the Loving Heart. Watercolour by G. Pieri Nerli, *c.* 1892. Lady Stair's House Museum, Edinburgh.

97 Feast held to celebrate the completion of the Road of the Loving Heart. Lady Stair's House Museum, Edinburgh.

98 Fanny Stevenson and a Samoan girl. Lady Stair's House Museum, Edinburgh.

99 Robert Louis Stevenson in bed, playing a flageolet. Lady Stair's House Museum, Edinburgh.

Diamond Head, Waikiki Beach. Pen-drawing by Robert Louis Stevenson. Silverado Museum, St Helena, California.

100 Illustration from 'The Bottle Imp', in Robert Louis Stevenson, *Island Nights' Entertainments* (1893). British Museum, London.

102 Robert Louis Stevenson. Oil-painting by G. Pieri Nerli, 1892–93. Scottish National Portrait Gallery, Edinburgh. Photo National Galleries of Scotland.

Robert Louis Stevenson's desk, Vailima. Silverado Museum, St Helena, California.

103 Robert Louis Stevenson dictating to Belle Strong, 1892. Lady Stair's House Museum, Edinburgh.

104 The Lammermuir Hills, seen from Dirleton Castle, East Lothian. Photo Edwin Smith.

106 Page from Robert Louis Stevenson's autograph manuscript of *Weir of Hermiston*, 1894. Trustees of the Pierpont Morgan Library, New York.

107 Lord Braxfield. Oil-painting by Henry Raeburn. Advocates Library, Edinburgh. Crown Copyright. Reproduced by permission of the Department of the Environment. Photo National Galleries of Scotland.

109 Robert Louis Stevenson lying in state, Vailima. Lady Stair's House Museum, Edinburgh.

110 Robert Louis Stevenson's tomb, Samoa. Mansell Collection.

111 One of the plaques on Robert Louis Stevenson's tomb, Samoa, inscribed with verses from Stevenson's poem 'Requiem'. Lady Stair's House Museum, Edinburgh.

113 Apia, Samoa, as it is today. Photo Bruce Moss.

114 Map. Drawn by Hanni Bailey.

116 Robert Louis Stevenson. Woodcut from *The Bookman*, 1913. British Museum, London.

INDEX